"*In his book* The Mi[...] [...] Fatima, *author John Preiss m[...] [...] today. Prayer, penance, conv[...] [...]nd can be practiced and lived not only by individuals but also by societies — indeed by countries — as a whole. What our Blessed Mother revealed to three shepherd children in 1917 echoes throughout the decades as a heavenly battle cry to save the world and all its peoples from self-destruction.*"

— *Father Wade Menezes, C.P.M., Fathers of Mercy Assistant General and EWTN Series Host*

"*In* The Miracle and the Message: 100 Years of Fatima, *John Preiss recounts a number of significant, mostly unknown, details which show that Fatima remains one of the most relevant messages for the world today. He demonstrates that Fatima is not simply a pious tale from the past, but a Message that re-presents the essential elements of the Gospel and motivates us to greater fidelity to God, who is Father, Son, and Holy Spirit. I recommend* The Miracle and the Message *to all who want to better live the Gospel.*"

— *Father Joseph M. Wolfe, M.F.V.A., Franciscan Missionaries of the Eternal Word*

"*Francisco and Jacinta Marto have been canonized — and the Servant of God Lucia Dos Santos advances toward the honors of the altar, as well — but the miracle and meaning of Fatima are far from over. The Fatima message remains as relevant today as when it was first given to the world one hundred years ago. In this wonderful book, John Preiss does a remarkable job of reminding us of the fundamentals of Fatima. In essence, Jesus and Mary continue to call us to repentance, prayer, and acts of reparation to the Eucharistic Presence of Our Lord and the Immaculate Heart of Our Lady.*"

— *Father Donald Calloway, M.I.C., S.T.L., author,* Champions of the Rosary: The History and Heroes of a Spiritual Weapon

THE MIRACLE AND THE MESSAGE
100 YEARS OF FATIMA

"Blessed By "Canon Tom
Lavin ... "Stationed At
"Knock Parish" — on
"Wednesday 17TH of November
20/21 -

The Miracle and the Message

100 Years of Fatima

John C. Preiss

Our Sunday Visitor

www.osv.com
Our Sunday Visitor Publishing Division
Our Sunday Visitor, Inc.
Huntington, Indiana 46750

Our Sunday Visitor Publishing Division, Our Sunday Visitor, Inc., 200 Noll Plaza, Huntington, IN 46750; 1-800-348-2440.

ISBN: 978-1-68192-167-9 (Inventory No. T1882)
eISBN: 978-1-68192-168-8
LCCN: 2017944648

Cover design by Tyler Ottinger

Cover photo: EPA PHOTO/Newscom
Cover background and photo on page 148: Shutterstock

Photos on pages 141–147 courtesy of Fatima Family Apostolate

PRINTED IN THE UNITED STATES OF AMERICA

About the Author

John Preiss is President of the Fatima Family Apostolate International, a Public Association of the Faithful, founded in 1986 by the late Father Robert J. Fox. The mission of the Fatima Family Apostolate International is to promote the message of Fatima and the sanctification of family life.

John is also the editor of the quarterly newsletter the *Fatima Family Messenger*. He has been interviewed on Catholic radio and on Vatican Radio about the consecration to the Immaculate Heart of Mary by Pope Francis. John has written several articles on the message of Fatima and the blessings of family life. He is also the author of *Our Lady of Fatima: True Devotion* and the children's book *The Miracle of the Dancing Sun at Fatima*. In the past John hosted a radio show called *Family Matters*.

John is an adult convert to the Catholic faith. He and his wife, Teresa, currently reside in Hanceville, Alabama, with their eight children (and counting): Mark, Lauren, Brenden, John David, Anna Sophia, Ella, Luke, and Angelica.

Dedication

I dedicate this book to Mary, Mother of the Church and Queen of Heaven and Earth. Mary's greatest desire is to bring souls to Her Beloved Son, Jesus.

My hope is that, through the messages of Our Lady and the example of the three humble shepherds, this book will bring you closer to Our Lord and Our Lady. Also, I pray that Fatima will become a part of your daily spiritual life by praying the Rosary, wearing the brown scapular, and making the Five First Saturdays devotion.

Finally, I acknowledge the late Father Robert J. Fox, without whom this book would have never become a reality.

May this book serve in some way to carry out to the world the mission given to us by Our Lady of Fatima.

John C. Preiss
President, Fatima Family Apostolate

CONTENTS

FATIMA:
A MESSAGE FOR THE WORLD

I can remember when I first heard about the apparitions at Fatima. I was in Father Robert J. Fox's living room. After writing several books and doing all he could to increase devotion to Our Lady of Fatima, Father Fox was known throughout the world as the "Fatima Priest."

I wondered at the time, "Why Fatima?" With all the countless devotions in the Church, why should a nearly one-hundred-year-old apparition to three shepherd children in Portugal have any special importance? Over time I came to realize the answer: Fatima is not just a place; it is a message and a call.

The message of Fatima is universal — a message for you and for me that reflects all the teachings of the Catholic Church. It is at once simple enough for children to understand and deep enough to baffle theologians. It is not simply directed to pilgrims or for those seeking Mary's intervention in specific areas of their lives. In fact, we don't have to go to Fatima to live out the Fatima message. The message of Fatima can become a part of our daily spiritual lives wherever we are. Simply put, the message of Fatima is that Mary, the Mother of Jesus Christ, is living, real, and present in our lives, interceding for us.

The call of Fatima is an invitation to embrace what Mary offers both the Church and the world. What does Mary want for us? A personal relationship with her Son, Jesus Christ. Mary *always* leads us to Jesus.

A century after the first apparition of Our Lady to Lucia, Francisco, and Jacinta in Fatima, Portugal, the message and the call live on. That is because what flows from Fatima is more than a Marian devotion: it is all at once centered on the Holy Trinity, focused on Christ, strengthening to the Church, and oriented toward prayerful union with God. The message of Fatima is not only for one time and place: it is just as urgent and relevant today as it was a century ago. Father Luciano Guerra, former rector of the Fatima shrine, writes:

> In the light of the face of Mary, which here [at the Fatima Shrine in Portugal] perhaps becomes more attractive, in the motherly warmth of her Immaculate Heart, in the simplicity of the children who had the grace of seeing and hearing her, certainly, also through individual and public manifestations of filial piety, which take place wherever Our Lady of Fatima is venerated, we are forced to hope that this grace, until today full of divine surprises, constitutes still today an abundant source of energy for the renovation of the Church, now that we have entered the third millennium.... The message irradiating from Fatima has the power of strengthening the faith, of purifying the hearts of the pilgrims and of getting them closer to God and their fellow men.[1]

Whenever the Blessed Virgin appeared at Fatima, she had a gold ball at her waist. People came to understand that this ball represented the world and signified that the message of Fatima was for the whole world. If we put ourselves in the place of Lucia, Francisco, and Jacinta, we too, can do what Our Lady asks of us. Through the

Fatima message, we can be shaped into what God desires for us, just as the humble shepherd children were.

We don't have to be especially "holy" or educated. The apparitions at Fatima prove that God chooses the simplest people to carry out his greatest works. Sister Lucia stated in later writings, "The Lord shows that the work is his and not that of weak instruments which he has chosen; for God it is enough that these instruments allow themselves to be molded and transformed and moved by the grace at work within them, engraving in their pure hearts and innocent hearts the reflections of his presence, the touches of His grace and the impulses of His love." God still wants to speak to us through Fatima. If we open ourselves up to him, a transformation of grace will take place.

The three most recent popes have recognized the urgency of the messages of Our Lady at Fatima for our world today. Pope Saint John Paul II developed a spiritual bond with Sister Lucia, one of the three little shepherds of the Fatima apparitions. He even donated the cornerstone, taken from Saint Peter's tomb beneath the Vatican, for the new Fatima church, which was dedicated on the ninetieth anniversary of the apparitions. This gift of the Holy Father was a sign of his deep conviction that he owed his life to Our Lady of Fatima, whom he credited for saving him from an assassination attempt on May 13, 1981. Pope Emeritus Benedict XVI entrusted his pontificate to the Virgin Mary at Fatima. Pope Francis has done the same.

The message of Fatima has unfolded over time, further confirming that it has lasting significance for us today. In his assessment of the Little Shepherds, the late Father Luis Kondor, S.V.D., former postulator for the canonizations of now Saints Francisco and Jacinta, noted: "The full content of the Fatima message and its mission was not given all at once at the time of the apparitions in 1917, but in the course of the various preliminary private and public interrogations of the visionaries." In fact, Lucia — the only one of the three seers to survive into adulthood — only wrote about the apparitions and the various messages of Our Lady when told to do so, many years after the apparitions occurred.

Father Kondor continued:

It is true that, immediately after the first apparition on May 13, 1917, articles, interrogations of the visionaries ... publications, periodicals, booklets and books began to make their appearance, and that all of these are now of great historical importance. Nevertheless, a great many writers wrote nothing because they lacked the necessary ecclesiastical authorization, which was not granted until October 13, 1930. This was the date on which D. José Alves Correia da Silva published Fatima's so-called "Magna Carta" in which he declared the apparitions worthy of credence and authorized the cult of Our Lady in the Cova da Iria. This authorization was of great importance for the literature concerning Fatima, beginning in fact with the writings of Sister Lucia, which we can classify as "source documents," since the other two visionaries had died before they learned how to write. One can state, to begin with, that Sister Lucia never wrote anything of her own volition. She wrote only when she was ordered to do so. Sister Lucia destroyed the first document concerning the Five First Saturdays of the month which she had written on December 10, 1925, shortly after she had received the vision described in it. The description we now have is, therefore, a second edition, sent to her spiritual director, Father Aparicio, S.J., on December 17, 1927. In it, Sister Lucia explains how she had received authorization from heaven to share the part of the Fatima "secret" relating to the devotion to the Immaculate Heart of Mary and the conditions required in order to respond to the call of the Five First Saturdays.[2]

Lucia produced this first document, long and very important, in obedience to D. José Alves Correia da Silva, bishop of the Diocese of Leiria. He had asked her to provide a spiritual portrait of Jacinta. In what is now known as Sister Lucia's first memoir, the apparitions provide no more than a framework. She finished the thirty-nine pages on Christmas Day, 1935.

Father Kondor writes further:

> The second document is a communication to Father Goncalves, S.J., who at the time was Sister Lucia's spiritual director. In it she describes the vision she received on June 13, 1929, when Our Lady asked the Pope, in union with all the Bishops of the world, to consecrate Russia to the Immaculate Heart of Mary, in order to attain the conversion of that country and peace for the world and peace within the hearts of man. There are also many letters, records of interrogations and reports."[3]

This second memoir was also written at the request of the Bishop of Leiria. Lucia's intention was to "reveal the story of Fatima just as it is." The seventy-six-page document was begun on November 7, 1937, and completed on November 21.

A third memoir of fifteen pages was written between the end of July and August 31, 1941. It reveals the first two parts of the Secret imparted by Our Lady on July 13, 1917: the vision of hell and God's desire for devotion to Mary's Immaculate Heart. Finally, a fourth memoir, again written at the request of Sister Lucia's superiors, was begun on October 7 and completed on December 8, 1941. This is how Sister Lucia's principal testimony came to be written.

Quite another matter, however, was the very slow way in which these writings were made known to the general public. As a result, the events of Fatima remained shrouded in secrecy and silence. Bishop D. José Alves Correia da Silva, however, instructed Sister Lucia to write down the best-kept third part of the "secret" in January 1944, when she was seriously ill and it was feared she might die. Responding to the bishop's request, Sister Lucia leaned against the mattress in her monastic cell, and wrote down four pages that documented the last part of the vision received by the three little shepherds on July 13, 1917.

This last part of Lucia's writings could well be entitled "The Great Martyrdom of the Church in the Twentieth Century." The document contains a prophetic description of an attempt against the life of Pope John Paul II which ultimately occurred on May 13, 1981, in Saint Peter's Square in Rome. This third part of the secret would not be revealed until the beatification of Francisco and Jacinta, on May 13, 2000. With its publication, the whole of Our Lady's message has been made known. There is nothing further to be revealed, as Sister Lucia herself declared shortly before she died.

When Sister Lucia was asked how she viewed the message over time, she stated:

> If the message was chosen by men, it would have been the first to be rejected. Think of it: for such a message, a rural hillside, a stony place, devoid of natural beauty, with no means of transport, without shelter of any kind to protect people from the hot sun in the summer or the torrential rain and storms in the winter. No one would go there! Often what men reject is what God chooses, because his is the power, the wisdom, the grace and energy that is at work in souls, moving them and carrying them as he wishes.[4]

While she was still living, many people longed for a face-to-face interview with Sister Lucia. Such meetings were almost never granted. In order to visit her at the cloistered Carmel in Coimbra where she lived, one needed a permit issued by the prefect of the Congregation for the Doctrine of the Faith. The prohibition against receiving visitors had been imposed on her to protect her life of prayer as a contemplative Carmelite nun. While Sister Lucia made use of every possible means for making the Blessed Virgin "better known and loved," she always abided by this order, despite the many people who wanted to see her. She did, however, receive thousands of letters over the eighty-eight years between the time of the apparitions and her death. When she discussed this with Pope Paul VI during his visit in 1967, he suggested she write a long letter in response, which became the book *"Calls" from the Message of Fatima* (*Apelos da Mensagem de Fatima*). "Calls" was published on December 13, 2000, on the authority of Pope John

Paul II and endorsed by the Congregation for the Doctrine of the Faith.

In *"Calls,"* Sister Lucia tells us that the first call that God addresses to us through Fatima is a call to faith:

> Faith is the basis of the entire spiritual life. It is by faith that we believe in the existence of God, in his power, his wisdom, his mercy, his work of redemption, his pardon and his fatherly love. It is by faith that we believe in God's Church, founded by Jesus Christ, and in the doctrine the Church transmits to us and by which we shall be saved. It is by the light of faith that we see Christ in others, loving, serving and helping them when they are in need of our assistance. And it is also our faith that assures us that God is present within us, that his eyes are always upon us.[5]

While Catholics are not required to believe in the extraordinary events that occurred at Fatima, those who do have found their faith renewed.

Fatima Today

Before the Blessed Virgin Mary appeared to the children at Fatima, they were visited by an angel. Sister Lucia would later recall:

> God began the preparation of the instruments that He had chosen when they, utterly carefree, were praying and playing, by causing to pass before their eyes, gently and slowly, what seemed to be white as snow in the shape of a human being. The purpose was to draw our attention to it.

And in fact, even to this day I don't know. But the events that followed make me believe that it must have been our Guardian angel who, without showing himself clearly, was preparing us for the accomplishment of God's plan.[6]

This first appearance of the Angel occurred in 1915. With no verbal message for the children, it made the children aware of the supernatural. God was preparing them for the incredible events that were about to unfold. This, too, has relevance for us today. God often allows us to be touched in a special way in order to help us to become more aware of his presence and how he is working in our lives.

Over the course of his visits, the Angel taught the children to pray in union with Christ present in the Eucharist. "The message of the Angel in the 'Loca do Cabeco,' as well as the way the shepherd children received him, is a pressing invitation for us today. It calls us to remember that adoration and consecration to the Most Holy Trinity are the end goal of our Christian life."[7]

Prayer is at the very heart of the message of Fatima because it is at the heart of growing in a personal relationship with God. From the first apparitions of the Angel, the children were asked to pray. When Our Lady appeared for six consecutive months in 1917, she asked the children to pray the Rosary every day for peace. Those of us living in the twenty-first century can take this request to heart. The peace Our Lady asks us to pray for is not only peace between nations, but peace within our hearts and homes. Now, more than ever, we need prayer.

The message of Fatima is a message of hope for all of us as we prepare for the coming triumph of Our Lady's

Immaculate Heart. It is a message that can be applied to our everyday lives of faith. As we look deeper into the meaning of these visits from the Angel of Peace and Our Lady, we will discover that Fatima is not just a nice, entertaining story. It is a message that can transform our spiritual lives if we are open to it. Fatima's message of prayer, penance, and sacrifice changed the lives of three shepherd children one hundred years ago. That very same message can strengthen us for our own spiritual journeys.

CHAPTER 1

FATIMA FROM THE BEGINNING

Three significant appearances of the Angel of Peace at Fatima took place in the spring, summer, and fall of 1916 — a year before the more famous apparitions of Mary. Lucia, Francisco, and Jacinta were playing games and watching their flocks at the time of the apparitions. They were simple, normal children. Francisco loved to play with sticks and throw rocks. Jacinta enjoyed dancing. Lucia, the oldest, was the ringleader. After playing, the children would say the Rosary but would modify it so that it would not last very long and they could resume playing. Many of us can relate to this. Sometimes we get too busy doing other things and avoid the things that are most important for us. In fact, the message the Angel brought to the children applies to us all.

How It All Began

According to Sister Lucia, the exact dates of the apparitions are not known: "At the time I did not know how to reckon the years, the months, or even the days of the week." However, by recalling the weather outside, she was able to indicate the season when each of the three apparitions took place.

When the Angel first appeared, Lucia had just turned nine, Francisco was barely eight, and Jacinta was only six years old. But why three simple children? If we consider the nature of children — their ability to absorb and retell a story in detail without any preconceived notions or agendas —

we can see how this works for God's plan. If the message of Fatima had been given to three adults, it may well have been distorted by pressures from the outside world.

"I Am the Angel of Peace"

One spring day, while tending their sheep in a property that was known as the Chousa, Lucia and her cousins, Jacinta and Francisco, had led their flock to the east side of a rocky outcropping known as the Cabeco. Here is Sister Lucia's account of the events that took place:

> Around the middle of the morning, a fine rain began to fall, so fine that it seemed like mist. We went up the hillside, followed by our flocks, looking for an overhanging boulder where we could take shelter. Thus it was for the first time that we entered this blessed hollow among the rocks. It stood in the middle of an olive grove belonging to my godfather Anastacio. From there, you could see the little village where I was born, my parents' home and the hamlets of Casa Velha and Eira da Pedra.
>
> We spent the day there among the rocks, in spite of the fact that the rain was over and the sun was shining bright and clear. We ate our lunch and said our Rosary.... A strong wind began to shake the trees. We looked up, startled, to see what was happening, for the day was unusually calm. Then we saw, coming towards us, above the olive trees … a young man, about fourteen or fifteen years old, whiter than snow, transparent as crystal when the sun shines through it, and of great beauty.

We were surprised, absorbed, and struck with amazement. On reaching us, he said: "Do not be afraid! I am the Angel of Peace. Pray with me."

Kneeling on the ground, he bowed down until his forehead reached the ground. Led by a supernatural impulse, we did the same, and repeated the words which we heard him say: "My God, I believe, I adore, I hope and I love Thee! I ask pardon of Thee for those who do not believe, do not adore, do not hope and do not love Thee!"

Having repeated these words three times, he rose and said: "Pray thus. The Hearts of Jesus and Mary are attentive to the voice of your supplications."

Then he disappeared.[8]

While we often forget and neglect the good angels who are here to help us on our path to eternity, devotion to the holy angels was very much alive in Portugal at that time. Morning and evening, the children were taught to invoke their guardian angels. So, this apparition was not completely surprising to the little shepherds. And what could be more in harmony with the great tradition of the apparitions of angels than the first words of the Angel of Fatima: "Fear not! I am the Angel of Peace." Later, when Sister Lucia was asked what the Angel was like, she answered simply: "He was Light."

Throughout Scripture, light attends God, His angels, and all holy beings. The angel who announced the resurrection of Christ had an appearance as of lightning, and his garment was white as snow (see Mt 28:3). Describing Our Lord transfigured on Mount Tabor, Saint Matthew tells us that "his face shone like the sun" (Mt 17:2), and "his clothes became dazzling white, such as no fuller on earth could bleach them" (Mk 9:3). Saint John says, "God is light, and in Him is no darkness at all" (1 Jn 1:5). Whenever God comes to manifest Himself to us by the ministry of angels or the mediation of Mary or any of the saints, He appears clothed in great splendor, as in this beautiful verse from the psalms: "LORD, my God, you are great indeed! / You are clothed with majesty and splendor, / robed in light as with a cloak" (Ps 104:1b–2).

After each of the apparitions at Fatima (which always took place at noon), this word "light" was always on the lips of the young seers. This sparkling light indicates the overwhelming presence of God, which leaves the natural senses almost paralyzed.

Sister Lucia details:

> The supernatural atmosphere which enveloped us was so intense that for a long time we were scarcely aware of our own existence, remaining in the same posture in which he had left us, and continually repeating the same prayer. The presence of God made itself felt so intimately and so intensely that we did not even venture to speak to one another. The next day, we were still immersed in this spiritual atmosphere, which only gradually began to disappear.
>
> It did not occur to us to speak about this Apparition, nor did we think of recommending that it be kept secret. The very Apparition itself imposed secrecy. It was so intimate, that it was not possible to speak of it at all. The impression it made upon us was all the greater perhaps, in that it was the first such manifestation we had experienced.[9]

The Angel taught the children a prayer in this first encounter: *My God, I believe, I adore, I hope, and I love you. And I ask pardon for those who do not believe, do not adore, do not hope, and do not love you.* This prayer can be seen as an introduction to our faith and how we are to share it with others. Faith is the foundation of our spiritual life. It is by faith that we encounter God within our hearts. At times, we may try to impose our faith on others and forget that we can only plant the seed; the Holy Spirit does the watering — and weeding. Faith is the gift of God.

Hope comes from our belief in God. When the Angel told the children, "Pray thus. The Hearts of Jesus and Mary are attentive to the voice of your supplications," he was encouraging them to hope. This message remains true in our day. We must be faithful and then humbly trust in the Hearts of Jesus and Mary to receive our prayers and carry them to our heavenly Father.

Sister Lucia tells us that Francisco did not have the privilege of hearing the words of the Angel; the others had to repeat them to him. Interestingly, this would remain the case for all the apparitions at Fatima. Yet Francisco was favored with the "essentials": the heavenly vision and the graces that the message of Fatima imparted to all the children's souls. For the Angel did not come merely to speak with them; he also came to fill them with special graces for the mission that was to come. Sister Lucia describes this:

> God sent his Angel with the message of peace and prayer, thereby introducing us into the climate of the supernatural, of faith, hope and love.[10]

The visit of the Angel also gave them peace and joy in God: "The peace and happiness which we felt were great, but wholly interior, for our souls were completely immersed in God. The physical weakness that came over us was also great." If we reflect on this, we see the work of God's mercy for all mankind, in all times and places. God desires to carry out his work in the world through us. God is always merciful; ready to forgive us as soon as we desire to amend our lives and are truly sorry. If we respond to the message of Fatima to pray, do penance, and make sacrifices for the offenses committed against God, especially in our society today, God will show His mercy to all people. At the same time, the Angel's message instructs us not only to amend our lives, but also to forgive our brothers and sisters.

"Pray, Pray Very Much!"

Sister Lucia described the Angel's second apparition:

> The second apparition must have been at the height of summer when the heat of the day was so intense that we had to take the sheep home before noon and only let them out again in the early evening. We went to spend the siesta hours in the shade of the trees which surrounded the well that I have already mentioned several times. Suddenly, we saw the same Angel right beside us.
>
> "What are you doing? Pray, pray very much! The Holy Hearts of Jesus and Mary have designs of mercy on you. Offer prayers and sacrifices constantly to the Most High."
>
> Lucia asked: "How are we to make sacrifices?"
>
> "Make of everything you can a sacrifice, and offer it to God as an act of reparation for the sins by which He is offended, and in supplication for

the conversion of sinners. You will thus draw down peace upon your country. I am its Angel Guardian, the Angel of Portugal. Above all, accept and bear with submission the suffering which the Lord will send you."[11]

After the request from the Angel, the three shepherd children participated in these designs of mercy. They obtained abundant graces for the Church and for all humankind throughout many years of tribulation and darkness. The children gave themselves totally to the Immaculate Heart, allowing their faith to be formed by Mary and embracing fully her mission to the world. As a result, they became great channels of mercy and conversion. They have left us a wonderful — and challenging — example. To imitate it in our own lives, we must become humble and obedient like little children so that we can receive and participate in God's merciful plan for salvation.

The lesson was not in vain, even in the short term. By autumn, when the Angel came for the last time, the children were no longer cutting their prayers short to play. Instead, they repeated the prayer which the Angel had taught them frequently, at times even lying prostrate on the ground. Francisco had not heard the Angel's words and could only understand them with difficulty when Lucia repeated them to him. Nevertheless, he was captivated by the beauty of the Angel and the intensity of the supernatural light that accompanied him.

"Console Your God"

Sister Lucia notes the time of the third apparition of the Angel: "The third apparition must have taken place in October, or toward the end of September, as we were no longer returning for siesta." On this day, the three shepherds had pastured their flocks at the Pregueira, a small olive grove that belonged to the dos Santos family, on the south side of the Cabeco. She continues:

> After our lunch, we decided to go and pray in the hollow among the rocks on the opposite side of the hill. To get there, we went around the slope, and had to climb over some rocks above the Pregueira. The sheep could only scramble over these rocks with great difficulty. As soon as we arrived there, we knelt down with our foreheads touching the ground, and began to repeat the prayer of the Angel: "My God, I believe, I adore, I hope and I love Thee...."
>
> I don't know how many times we repeated this prayer, when an extraordinary light shone upon us. We sprang up to see what was happening, and beheld the Angel. He was holding a chalice in his left hand, with the Host suspended above it, from which some drops of Blood fell into the chalice. Leaving the chalice suspended in the air, the Angel knelt down beside us and made us repeat three times:
>
> "Most Holy Trinity, Father, Son and Holy Ghost, I offer Thee the most precious Body, Blood, Soul and Divinity of Jesus Christ, present in all the tabernacles of the world, in reparation for the sacrileges, outrages and indifferences by which He Himself is offended. And through the infinite merits of His Most Sacred Heart, and the Immaculate Heart of Mary, I beg of Thee the conversion of poor sinners."

Then, rising, he took the chalice and the Host in his hands. He gave the Sacred Host to me, and shared the Blood from the chalice between Jacinta and Francisco, saying as he did so: "Take and drink the Body and Blood of Jesus Christ, horribly outraged by ungrateful men! Make reparation for their crimes and console your God."

Once again, he prostrated on the ground and repeated with us, three times more, the same prayer "Most Holy Trinity ..." and then disappeared.

Moved by a supernatural force which enveloped us, we had imitated the Angel in everything; that is, we prostrated as he did and repeated the prayers that he said.... We remained a long time in this position, repeating the same words over and over again. It was Francisco who realized that it was getting dark, and drew our attention to the fact, and thought we should take our flocks back home. I felt that God was in me.[12]

Sister Lucia later said love for the Eucharist was the most important part of the message of Fatima for the children. This drew them closer to God and instilled in their hearts the importance of the real presence of Christ in the Holy Eucharist. For us today, the entire message of the Angel contains an urgent call to prayer, sacrifice, and reparation for sin to the Most Holy Trinity and our Eucharistic Lord.

Lucia again recorded the state of physical exhaustion into which the angelic apparition plunged them:

In the third apparition, the presence of the Angel was still more intense. For several days, even Francisco did not dare to talk. He said later on: "I love to see the Angel, but the trouble is that later on, we are incapable of doing anything. I could not even walk any more. I didn't know what was the matter!"

It was a grace so sublime, and so intimate, that Francisco, all absorbed in God, did not have a clear consciousness of the mystical grace that he had received and felt in a confused way. Once the first few days were over, and we had returned to normal, Francisco asked: "The Angel gave you Holy Communion, but what was it that he gave to Jacinta and me?" "It was Holy Communion, too," replied Jacinta, with inexpressible joy. "Didn't you see that it was the Blood that fell from the Host?" Francisco replied: "I felt that God was within me, but I did not know how!"

From this moment on, we had begun to offer God everything that mortified us, but without looking to impose particular penances on ourselves, except to pass entire hours prostrated on the ground, repeating the prayer which the Angel had taught us.... We remained prostrate a long time, sometimes repeating these prayers even to the point of exhaustion.

Afterwards, when we prostrated to say that prayer, Francisco was the first to feel the strain of such a posture; but he remained kneeling, or sitting, and still praying until we had finished. Later he said: "I am not able to stay like that for a long time, like you. My back aches so much that I can't do it."[13]

However, God Himself would send His willing children the most fruitful sacrifices. The trials that would overwhelm Lucia's family coincided almost exactly with the time of the first few apparitions. Little by little, her home life grew unhappy. This was all the more painful for Lucia because, until then, she had known great joy in her family, whom she tenderly cherished and who cherished her in return.

Sister Lucia notes:

> Although I was only a child, I understood perfectly the situation we were in. Then I remembered the Angel's words: "Above all, accept submissively the sacrifices that the Lord will send you."
>
> At such times, I used to withdraw to a solitary place, so as not to add to my mother's suffering by letting her see my own. This place, usually, was our well. There, on my knees, leaning over the edge of the stone slabs that covered the well, my tears mingled with the water below and I offered my suffering to God. Sometimes, Jacinta and Francisco would come and find me like this, in bitter grief. As my voice was choked with sobs and I couldn't say a word, they shared my suffering to such a degree that they also wept copious tears.[14]

These difficult trials did not leave the shepherd children overwhelmed, however; the Angel had told the children about these sufferings and had invited them to offer them in reparation for sins, for the consolation of God, and for the conversion of sinners.

The children received a very special grace, and the words of the Angel had entered their souls in a profound way. As Sister Lucia explains:

These words were indelibly impressed upon our minds. They were like a light which made us understand Who God is, how He loves us and desires to be loved, the value of sacrifice, how pleasing it is to Him and how, on account of it, He gives the grace of conversion to sinners. It was for this reason that we began, from then on, to offer to the Lord all that mortified us.[15]

Through these three apparitions, the Angel taught the humble shepherd children how to pray and offer their sacrifices. Francisco and Jacinta were deeply touched and grew in the spiritual life. The Angel also prepared them for what was to come. For Sister Lucia, the apparitions of the Angel remained the most important parts of the message of Fatima. Sister Lucia wrote: "The message is more a new light to shine in the midst of darkness. Great is the Lord, immense in His mercy, eternal in His love! I believe in Thee, I adore Thee. I trust and I love Thee! For Thee I live!"

Chapter 2

Visits from Our Lady
(May–September)

In central Portugal the terrain is rocky, and the soil is very poor. The summers are extremely dry, and it seldom rains. Olive oil is the chief marketable commodity for the farmers, so it is especially tragic when fire destroys large numbers of olive trees.

In June, the farmers harvest wheat; in early fall, corn and grapes. In August of each year, on the 13th, hundreds of farmers bring sacks of wheat to the basilica at the Cova da Iria, to donate for use in making flour for altar breads for the following year. These breads, the humble farmers know, will be consecrated into the Body of Christ and distributed at Masses celebrated during the coming year for the teeming pilgrims who will come to Fatima.

The Basilica of Our Lady of the Rosary stands atop the hill where Lucia, Francisco, and Jacinta played games while herding their sheep. It is there that they encountered Our Lady for the first time. As we recount the apparitions, imagine that you are one of the three shepherds on that hill, and Our Lady is appearing to you.

May Apparition

In spite of the Angel's earlier apparitions, the three children never assumed that anything of great significance would happen again. They had the sheep up on the family property called the Cova da Iria and were playing as usual when all of a sudden it happened.

This is how Sister Lucia described that first appearance of Our Lady on May 13, 1917:

> While playing with Jacinta and Francisco on the hilltop in the Cova da Iria, making a little stone wall around a furze-like clump called *moita*, suddenly we saw a flash of lightning. "There is a flash of lightning," I said to my cousins, "a thunder-storm may come on. It would be better for us to go home." "Oh yes, of course," they said. And we began to descend the hill driving the sheep along towards the road. When we reached a large holm-oak about halfway down the slope the light flashed again. Then a few paces further on, we beheld a beautiful lady dressed in white, poised over a holm-oak sapling very near us. She was more brilliant than the sun, radiating a sparkling light. Struck with amazement, we halted before this vision. We were so near that we were bathed in the light that radiated from her person to a distance of about three feet.
>
> Then the Lady said: "Do not be afraid; I will do you no harm."
>
> "Where are you from?" I asked.
>
> "I am from heaven."
>
> "What do you want of me?"
>
> "I came to ask you to come here for six successive months, on the 13th day at the same hour. Later I will tell what I want. And I will return here yet a seventh time."
>
> "And I, shall I go to heaven?"
>
> "Yes, you will."
>
> "And Jacinta?"
>
> "She will go also."

"And Francisco?"

"He will go there too, but he must say many Rosaries first."

Then I remembered to ask about two girls who had died recently. They were friends of mine and used to come to my home to learn weaving with my eldest sister. "Is Maria das Neves in heaven?"

"Yes, she is."

"And Amelia?"

"She will be in purgatory until the end of the world." (It seems to me that she was between 18 and 20 years of age.)[16]

"End of the world" is properly interpreted as a very long time. This was because people were not praying for her. In this moment, Our Lady confirmed the existence of purgatory. Her words to the children are a reminder to us that we should not forget to pray for the poor souls there. Sister Lucia continued with Mary's words:

"Do you wish to offer up to God all the sufferings He desires to send you in reparation for the sins by which he is offended, and in supplication for the conversion of sinners?"

"Yes, we do."

"Go then, for you will have much to suffer, but the grace of God will comfort you."

While pronouncing the words "the grace of God," Our Lady opened her hands for the first time, shedding on us a light so intense that it seemed as a reflex glancing from her hands and penetrating to the innermost recesses of our hearts, making us see ourselves in God, who was that Light, more clearly than we could see ourselves in a mirror. Then by an interior impulse, also communicated to us, we fell upon our knees, repeating in our hearts: "Oh, most Holy Trinity, I adore Thee! My God, my God, I love Thee in the most Blessed Sacrament!"[17]

This first apparition of Mary occurred on the Church's Feast of Our Lady of the Eucharist, and already the Mother of God was drawing the children to adore our Lord in the Holy Eucharist. As our heavenly Mother, Mary desires to lead all her children closer to the Eucharistic heart of Jesus, our food for eternal life.

After a few moments, Our Lady spoke to the children again: "Say the Rosary every day in order to obtain peace for the world and the end of the war." Sister Lucia then describes the end of the apparition:

> Then she began to ascend serenely, going up towards the east, the light that surrounded her seeming to open up a path before her, until she finally disappeared in the immensity of space, the reason why we sometimes said we saw heaven opening.[18]

On their way home after the apparition, the children decided not to tell anyone about the Lady they had seen. Jacinta was so impressed by the Lady's beauty, however, that she was unable to keep quiet, and told her mother about their encounter with the Mother of God. News spread quickly through the small village. While some were predisposed to believe the children's story, others immediately dismissed it as childish imagination, a bid for attention, or lies. Over the months that followed, many more people heard about what was happening in Fatima and the crowds grew.

The message of this first apparition was not only for three shepherd children in 1917; it is for all of us, even today. Mary's message to the children at Fatima invites us to offer up our sufferings for the conversion of sinners. Every one of us has something to offer on a daily basis. Our Lady also asks us to pray the Rosary for peace. The response we give is up to each one of us.

June Apparition

Our Lady appeared to the three little shepherds for the second time on June 13, 1917. June is the month traditionally devoted to the Sacred Heart of Jesus. In the June apparition, Mary urged that her Immaculate Heart be honored along with devotion to the Sacred Heart.

Lucia, the only one of the three children to speak directly with Mary, greeted the heavenly Lady each time, May through October, with the same words: "What do you want of me?"

Each time Our Lady emphasized: "I want you to pray the Rosary every day."

During this second apparition, Lucia told Our Lady: "I want you to take us to heaven."

The response was: "Yes, I will take Jacinta and Francisco soon, but you must remain here some time longer. Jesus wishes to make use of you to make me known and loved. He wants to establish devotion to my Immaculate Heart in the world."

Lucia, saddened that her two cousins would die soon, asked, "Must I stay here alone?"

Our Blessed Mother replied: "Do not be disheartened. I will never leave you. My Immaculate Heart will be your refuge and the way that will lead you to God." As Mary said these words, she opened her hands, and an immense light enveloped her. In this light, the three children saw themselves overwhelmed with the presence of God. Jacinta and Francisco were in the light focused on heaven. Lucia was in the light that beamed out over the earth. In front of the palm of Mary's right hand was a heart encircled with thorns that pierced it. The children understood this to be the Immaculate Heart of Mary, grieved by the sins of humanity.

The meaning of Our Lady's second apparition is timeless. Mary's request of Lucia, to make devotion to her Immaculate Heart known to the world, is for us, too. Francisco and Jacinta died within a little more than two years' time after the apparitions. Sister Lucia lived until February 13, 2005, and was nearly ninety-eight years of age. Her mind remained clear on the events surrounding the apparitions and the apparitions themselves, despite her age. For more than eighty-seven years after the apparitions, Jesus used her witness to establish devotion in the world to Mary's Immaculate Heart. We in the Church today are called to make devotion to Mary part of how we live our faith and to share it in any way we can. Mary is the model of Christian discipleship, and of everything the Church is and hopes to become. Her Immaculate Heart reflects perfect faith, hope, and love, the virtues that make us most like Christ.

Sister Lucia spoke of the call to all Christians in the message at Fatima: "Through your prayers, your words, your example, your acts of self denial, your work and your charity, you will be able to help your brothers and sisters to get up again if they have fallen, to return to the right path if they have strayed away from it, and to draw close to God if they are estranged from Him.... Very often, people are overcome and fall because they have no one at their side willing to pray and to make sacrifices for them, stretching out a hand to them, and helping them to follow a better path."[19]

The children kept the vision of Mary's heart secret. As Lucia later explained, "This is what we referred to, when we said that Our Lady had told us a secret in June. Our Lady did not order us to keep it a secret on this occasion, but we felt moved to do so by God."[20]

July Apparition

Today, so many have lost faith in the very existence of God. Many also have little or no belief in the reality of hell. Yet in the July apparition, the three little shepherd children were shown a vision of hell so terrible that Sister Lucia wrote that if they had not been promised they would all go to heaven, she thought they would have died on the spot.

A few moments after arriving at the Cova near the holm-oak tree, where a large number of people were already praying the Rosary, the little shepherds saw the flash of light, and Our Lady appeared over the tree a moment later. Lucia immediately asked, as she did each time Our Lady appeared, "What do you want of me?"

Mary replied, "I want you to come here on the 13th of next month. Continue to say the Rosary every day, in honor of Our Lady in order to obtain peace for the world and the end of the war because only she can obtain it."

Ten-year-old Lucia then made some requests of our Blessed Mother, which people had asked her to make. Our Lady responded that it was necessary for those persons to pray the Rosary in order to obtain the graces they were asking for during the year. Mary continued: "Sacrifice yourselves for sinners, and say often, especially when you make some sacrifice: 'O Jesus, this is for love of you, for the conversion of sinners, and in reparation for the sins committed against the Immaculate Heart of Mary.'"

Saying these last words, Our Lady opened her hands, as she had done the two previous months. It was at that moment that the children had a vision of hell. Sister Lucia described the vision in these words:

> The light from them [Our Lady's hands] seemed to penetrate the earth, and we saw a sea of fire. Plunged in this fire were demons and souls that looked like transparent embers, some black or bronze, in human form, driven about by the flames that issued from within themselves together with clouds of smoke. They were falling on all sides, just as sparks cascade from great fires, without weight or equilibrium, amid cries of pain and despair which horrified us so that we trembled with fear. It must have been this sight which caused me to cry out, as the people say they heard me exclaim aloud. The demons could be distinguished by their likeness to terrible, loathsome and unknown animals, transparent as live coals. Terrified and as if to plead for succour, we raised our eyes to Our Lady, who said to us kindly but sadly: "You have seen hell where the souls of poor sinners go. In order to save them, God wishes to establish in the world devotion to my Immaculate Heart. If you do what I tell you, many souls will be saved, there will be peace. The war will end, but if men do not cease offending God, another and more terrible war will break out during the pontificate of Pius XI. When you see a night lit up by an unknown light, know that it is

the sign God gives you that he is about to punish the world for its crimes by means of war, hunger, and persecution of the Church and the Holy Father. In order to prevent this, I shall come to ask for the consecration of Russia to my Immaculate Heart, and the Communion of reparation on the first Saturdays. If my wishes are fulfilled, Russia will be converted and there will be peace. If not, Russia will spread her errors throughout the world, promoting wars and persecution of the Church. The good will be martyred, the Holy Father will have much to suffer, and various nations will be annihilated. But in the end, my Immaculate Heart will triumph. The Holy Father will consecrate Russia to me and it will be converted, and a time of peace will be conceded to the world. In Portugal, the Dogma of Faith will always be preserved. Do not tell this to anybody. You may tell it to Francisco. When you recite the Rosary, after each mystery say: 'O my Jesus, forgive us [our sins], save us from the fire of hell, lead all souls to heaven, especially those who are most in need [of your mercy]."[21]

The July apparition, with its further call for devotion to the Immaculate Heart of Mary, reminds us to live a life of Christian virtue, as Mary did. To make a personal consecration to Mary's Immaculate Heart, we must follow the Ten Commandments, receive the sacraments worthily and in reparation to the Sacred Heart of Jesus and the Immaculate Heart Mary, and observe daily prayer, especially the Rosary. Our Lady warned that if we do not answer heaven's call, much chastisement will befall the world: "war, hunger, and persecution of the Church and the Holy Father."

While God's mercy is infinite, so is His justice. Through our cooperation, or lack thereof, we make the choice. God respects our free will to accept or refuse Him. For God's infinite mercy through the precious blood of Jesus, faith, repentance, and openness to his merciful love are required. Otherwise His justice must prevail. At Fatima, Mary introduced the First Saturday devotion along with consecration to her Immaculate Heart as a means to prevent the punishment due the world.

At Fatima, Mary warned us there would be a loss of faith throughout the world. We are now witnesses to what Mary prophesied. But all hope is not lost. The words of Our Lady during the July apparition show us how to return to Jesus. Mary invites us, as she urged the three shepherd children in July 1917, to seek God in union with her Immaculate Heart and to pray the Rosary daily.

Finally, after a short silence which followed, Lucia asked Our Lady: "Is there anything more that you want of me?"

"No, I do not want anything more of you today." And as in the previous apparitions, the beautiful Lady from heaven began to ascend toward the east, until she finally disappeared in the infinity of space.

Many people besides the three children felt a supernatural presence during the apparitions. To take one example, Mr. Antonio Marques shared his experience from July 13: "As an unbeliever I wanted to deny everything that I see, but looking on the atmosphere, I see everything is dark. It seems as if two opposing currents of air are at a meeting place, raising a cloud of dust. The weather becomes dark and I seem to hear an underground thunder. I feel the ambience is supernatural and I am afraid of being there."[22]

August Apparition

On August 13, the day the three children expected to meet Our Lady as they had promised, the administrator of Ourem deceptively took them away by horse cart. He pretended that he wanted to take the children to the Cova da Iria for the apparition. Instead, he took them to Ourem, where he placed them in jail with male prisoners and threatened to throw them into boiling oil if they did not admit that they were lying, or tell the secrets they said they had received.

As eventually revealed years later, the secret had three parts: first, the terrible vision of hell; second, God's desire to establish in the world devotion to the Immaculate Heart of his Mother in order to save souls; third, the many martyrs for the faith in the twentieth century and the suffering of the pope.

On that day in August 1917, however, the children refused to reveal anything to the administrator, and even compelled the men in prison to kneel in prayer with them. Seven-year-old Jacinta was especially courageous. Lucia wrote years later that she believed Jacinta received special grace to understand devotion to the Immaculate Heart of Mary. Even in prison, the little shepherds offered sacrifices for the conversion of sinners, as they were accustomed to do, instructed as they had been by the Angel and Our Lady. Jacinta prayed, "O my Jesus! This is for love of you, for the conversion of sinners, for the Holy Father, and in reparation for the sins committed against the Immaculate Heart of Mary." For remaining loyal in threat of death, the children have been considered "dry," or bloodless, martyrs.

Meanwhile, a crowd of people gathered at the holm-oak tree in the Cova, where Our Lady had been appearing at noon on the 13th of each month. While the children were not there, Our Lady nonetheless kept her appointment. Some of the onlookers saw mysterious signs, such as a pillar of blue cloud over the holm-oak, which appeared and disappeared three times. This told them Our Lady had come.

After the children were released from prison, Our Lady appeared to them on August 19 at a place called Valinhos, which is near the village Aljustrel. This village is within the parish of Fatima, and where the children lived with their families. Sister Lucia described the August 19 apparition this way:

> We were with the sheep in a place called Valinhos, Francisco and his brother John accompanying me, when I felt something supernatural approaching and enveloping us. Suspecting that Our Lady was coming, and feeling sorry that Jacinta should miss seeing her, we asked her brother John to go and call her. As he did not want to go, I offered him two coins and he ran off. Meanwhile, Francisco and I saw the flash of light which we called lightning, and a few moments after Jacinta's arrival, we saw Our Lady above a holm-oak.[23]

Our Lady appeared over a meter-high holm-oak tree as she had in the Cova da Iria.

As usual Lucia asked, "What do you want of me?"

"I want you to continue going to the Cova da Iria on the 13th, and to continue saying the Rosary every day. In the last month, I will perform a miracle so that all may believe." It was the second time Our Lady promised a miracle in October.

Lucia asked: "What do you want done with the money the people leave at the Cova da Iria?"

"Have two litters made with it, one for you and Jacinta to carry with two other girls dressed in white, the other for Francisco to carry with three other boys. The money placed on the litters is for the Feast of Our Lady of the Rosary, and what is over is to help towards the building of a chapel."

Lucia petitioned, "I wish to ask you to cure some sick persons."

Our Lady replied, "Yes, I will cure some of them during the year." And then with a sad expression she said, "Pray, pray very much and make sacrifices for sinners, for many souls go to hell because they have nobody to pray and make sacrifices for them." And Our Lady began to ascend as usual toward the east. Sister Lucia said she could never forget the sadness in Our Lady's voice when she made this request that August.

During each of the six apparitions at Fatima, Our Lady requested that the Rosary be prayed every day. This is different from the apparitions at Lourdes, France. When Mary appeared to Bernadette Soubirous at Lourdes in 1858, the rosary was on her elbow; yet at Fatima it was in her hands and always on her lips. Our Lady also appeared to little Jacinta in the parish church, showing her the mysteries of the Rosary, so that Jacinta might learn how to meditate on the mysteries.

During the August apparition, Mary urged the children to pray and sacrifice for the conversion of sinners who have no one else to pray for them. When we think of the events of our own times, we can understand why Pope John Paul II said, "Fatima is more relevant today than ever."

September Apparition

By September, the apparitions had ceased to be a local event. The news of Our Lady's appearances had spread far throughout Portugal. Many people travelled to the Cova da Iria on September 13, 1917, hoping for help and even healing of physical and spiritual illnesses. September would be a turning point for many to accept that the Blessed Virgin Mary was truly appearing to the children. At least twenty-five thousand people gathered at this apparition. In fact, the children's imprisonment in August had backfired for the administrator, as it helped make the events of Fatima more widely known.

The roads were packed with people. "For the love of God, ask Our Lady to cure my crippled son!" one parent cried. Another, "And mine, who is blind!" Yet another, "And mine who is deaf!" "That my son and my husband return from the war!" "That Our Lady convert me, a sinner!" "That she cure me of tuberculosis!" and so on. The roads were so full that the children could advance only because some gentlemen kept opening a path for them. Sister Lucia described it this way:

> Every element of poor humanity seemed to be there. Some climbed up into the trees or to the tops of walls to see us go by. We tried to answer some of the people, and to help others to rise from the dust where they were kneeling. It was due to some gentlemen, who kept opening a passage for us in the crowd, that we managed to move forward. Now when I read about those enchanting

scenes in the New Testament of the passing of Our Lord through Palestine, I think of our poor roads and lanes of Aljustrel, Fatima and Cova da Iria, and give thanks to God, offering him the faith of our good Portuguese people. And I think that if they could abase themselves like that before three poor children, just because they were mercifully granted the grace to speak to the Mother of God, what would they not do if they saw Our Lord Himself in person before them?[24]

Amidst the crowd in the Cova da Iria that September day was the well-known priest and theologian Father Manuel Nunes Formigao. Devoted to Lourdes, this expert in all things Marian was incredulous about the reports coming out of Fatima. He went to investigate, both as a theologian and as a lawyer. At the time of the apparition, the sun, as always, diminished in intensity, while people witnessed various phenomena. Some claimed to see a star come down to settle on the holm-oak tree; others saw a globe move from the east to the tree. The crowd witnessed flowers falling like rain drops; people tried to catch them with their hands or umbrellas, only to have them disappear.

Meanwhile, Our Lady appeared on the holm-oak.

Lucia asked, "What do you want of me?"

Our Lady spoke: "Continue to say the Rosary in order to obtain the end of the war. In October, Our Lord will come, and also Our Lady of Sorrows and Our Lady of Carmel. Saint Joseph will appear with the Child Jesus to bless the world. God is pleased with your sacrifices, but He does not want you to sleep with the cord on, only to wear it during the daytime."

Lucia said: "I was told to ask you many things: for the cure of some sick people, of a deaf mute...."

"Yes, I will cure some, but not others. In October I will perform a miracle so that all may believe." And then the beautiful lady from heaven began to ascend as usual to the east, and disappeared.

When it was over, Father Formigao was in deep prayer on his knees, saying, "It is true. It is true. Our Lady is appearing here." He became known as the fourth seer of Fatima. Eventually named to the diocese's canonical commission, he was officially entrusted to study the events in Fatima. This renowned expert, who had come to expose the "hoax," became one of Fatima's leading apostles and the one who initiated many of the original devotional practices at Fatima that are conducted to this day.

Over the course of Mary's apparitions, the children were changing their behavior and growing in faith, including in the spirit of penance. Especially after their vision of hell in July, the three children would give their lunches to poor children, abstain from water on hot days, wear rough cords around their waists, and bow low in adoration while offering the prayers taught them by the Angel in 1916. Francisco was almost constantly praying the Rosary.

The great appeal for prayer and penance that Our Lady gave at Fatima applies to us as well. Mary is asking us to do our part as members of the Body of Christ. We are also called to do our part to help fulfill the promise of the triumph of the Immaculate Heart by loving one another and offering up whatever we suffer for each other.

CHAPTER 3

THE MIRACLE OF THE SUN (OCTOBER 13, 1917)

When she appeared to the children in July, Our Lady promised a miracle in October. She foretold not just the miracle, but the exact day and hour. While she had not told the children the nature of the miracle, she did reveal three things to them: "In October I will tell you [1] who I am and [2] what I want, and [3] I will perform a miracle so that all may believe."[25]

On October 13, Lucia's mother accompanied her ten-year-old daughter for the first time, fearing that Lucia would be harmed if a miracle did not take place. Heavy rains had fallen since the evening before into the morning hours, and dark clouds hung over Fatima. Hoping to avoid delays along the way caused by all the masses of people, they left home early.

Despite the torrential rain, people were gathered all along the road. Lucia wrote: "My mother, fearing it would be the last day of my life and pierced to the heart by the uncertainty of what might happen, wanted to accompany me. She was so fearful that she even encouraged me to go to confession before we left for the Cova."[26] The scenes of the previous month were repeated along the way to the Cova, only people were even more numerous. Though reporters had told the story about the apparitions, they had never intended to encourage people to make a pilgrimage. There were even rumors of a possible attack at the site. But none of this mattered; the people kept coming.

The nasty, mud-filled roads did not prevent them from kneeling before the little shepherds in the humblest and most suppliant posture.

Upon reaching the holm-oak in the Cova da Iria, moved by an interior impulse, Lucia asked the people to close their umbrellas and pray the Rosary. The rain, which had continued to fall steadily since the night before, stopped suddenly — almost as if a faucet had been shut off — at the exact hour of noon. The clouds suddenly moved back from east to west. Our Lady arrived precisely on time. The children saw the flash of light, and Lucia cried: "Silence! Our Lady is coming!" From that moment on, the three children were not conscious of anything happening around them. They were totally absorbed by the apparition. Again, as in past visits, Lucia asked, "What do you want of me?"[27]

Our Lady answered, "I want to tell you that a chapel is to be built here in my honor, for I am the Lady of the Rosary. Continue always to pray the Rosary every day. The war will soon end, and the soldiers will return to their homes." When Lucia presented petitions on behalf of certain people, she received the answer: "Some yes, but not others. They must amend their lives and ask forgiveness for their sins." Then with a sad expression on her face: "Do not offend God Our Lord any more, for He is already deeply offended."[28]

The sorrowful look and sad tone of Mary's voice remained vivid in Lucia's memory to the end of her life. Still today, we know that many people continue to sin rather than seeking to live in grace. How can we expect God to help us if we do not live according to His word? At Fatima, Our Lady made clear that we must ask for forgiveness and be willing to change how we live. Often, we want to be helped but do not want to do what is necessary to receive the graces God wants to give us. Fatima makes clear that conversion is our personal responsibility. At the same time, we see at Fatima that, through Our Lady, we can grow closer to God.

After she finished speaking, the Mother of God opened her hands. Their image reflected on the sun. She then ascended, as the reflection of light emanating from her own body continued to be projected onto the sun itself. Lucia later said: "That is the reason why I cried aloud 'Look at the sun.' My intention was not to call the attention of the people to it, because I was not conscious of their presence. I was guided to do so by an interior impulse."[29]

The little shepherds then beheld, near the sun, the promised visions. Saint Joseph and the Child Jesus, making the Sign of the Cross with their hands, were blessing the world. Nearby was Our Lady, robed in white with a blue mantle. This vision vanished. Next, they saw Jesus and Mary as Our Lady of Sorrows. Our Lord, now appearing as a man, began to bless the world in the same manner as had Saint Joseph. Next appeared Mary under the title of Our Lady of Mount Carmel, holding the brown scapular down to the world. Lucia later interpreted that this indicated the Blessed Mother's desire for people to wear the brown scapular as a sign of their consecration to her Immaculate Heart.

The people stood bareheaded and pallid with fear, searching the sky as the sun "trembled" and made quick, startling movements. This phenomenon would come to be described as the miracle of the dancing sun. While the crowds experienced this solar display, Lucia stated that everything around reflected all the colors of the rainbow.

Thousands were utterly terrified by what they saw. After about ten minutes, the sun resumed its regular place. Relieved, the crowds began to sing joyously to Our Lady.

As the miracle came to its end and the people rose from the muddy ground, another surprise awaited them. Despite standing for so long in the soaking rain and mud, their clothes were perfectly dry. Many of the people had put on their best clothes to honor the Mother of Jesus; in return she provided them with this last little miracle.

It was not only devout Catholics who witnessed the miracle. Reporters and skeptics from far and wide had also come to the Cova that day see what would happen. Avelino de Almeda, who had been assigned as a special reporter for the anticlerical daily *O Seculo*, wrote: "The sun looked like a plaque of dull silver, and it was possible to look at it without the least discomfort. It neither burned nor blinded the eyes.… At that moment, a great shout went up, and one could hear the spectators nearest at hand shouting: 'A miracle! A miracle! A marvel! A marvel!' The sun, spinning as a giant Catherine wheel, descended three times as if it were going to crash into the people. It gave off all shades of colors. Then ascending back to its place in the sky, it descended again three times over a period of about ten minutes. Thinking the end of the world had come, some prayed aloud for forgiveness of their sins. Others exclaimed, "O Jesus! We are all going to die!… Our Lady, help us!"[30]

A reporter from a Lisbon newspaper saw it this way:

> The silver sun, enveloped in the same gauzy grey light, was seen to whirl and turn in the circle of broken clouds.… The light turned a beautiful blue, as if it had come through the stained glass windows of a cathedral, and spread itself over the people who

knelt with outstretched hands … in the presence of a miracle they had awaited. The seconds seemed like hours.[31]

The miracle of the sun remains one of the most spectacular miracles recorded in the two thousand-year history of the Church. It was heaven's verification of the message that the Mother of God came to deliver to the world at Fatima.

The October miracle was witnessed by an estimated seventy thousand people. It was not a magic trick designed to impress people, but served a deeper divine purpose. Just as the miracles of Jesus in the New Testament were signs given to bring people to faith with a response in love, the miracle of Fatima occurred to bring people to faith, to repentance, and to love for one another. Mary revealed herself as Our Lady of the Rosary, and had specific messages for the Church and the world, which can be recognized in the miracle itself. The most relevant messages for today are invitations to make family life holy, pray the Rosary daily, and consecrate one's self to the Immaculate Heart of Mary.

Sanctification of the family. The apparition at Fatima on October 13, 1917, is the only approved apparition in two thousand years in which the entire Holy Family (Jesus, Mary, and Joseph) appeared together at the same time. Many believe that Our Lady of Sorrows appearing with the Holy Family in this apparition was a prophetic sign of the breakdown of family life as God created it and intended it to be.

Sister Lucia wrote much on the family in her book *Fatima in Lucia's Own Words, Volume II, 5th and 6th Memoirs*, released in April 1999. She did the same, but more profoundly, quoting much Scripture, in her later book, *"Calls" from the Message of Fatima*, released in 2000 and recently translated into several languages. Published by permission of Pope Saint John Paul II, *"Calls" from the Message of Fatima* can be viewed as a catechism of Fatima. In the preface, Father Jesús Castellano Cervera, O.C.D., states: "The entire message of Fatima is a *great call to holiness for the Church of our time.* Lucia sees this call to holiness in some of the details of the apparition. The presence of Saint Joseph in one of apparitions is a pressing invitation to the sanctification of the family, a key theme throughout Lucia's book."[32] Sister Lucia entitled the eighteenth chapter of the book, "The Call to the Sanctification of the Family." Fatima is full of inspiration for the family to live in holiness and profess the totality of true faith.

Especially in her final years, Lucia focused on the holiness that should be in every family, as she wrote:

> In times such as the present, when the family often seems misunderstood in the form in which it was established by God, and is assailed by doctrines that are erroneous and contrary to the purposes for which the divine Creator instituted it, surely God wished to address to us a reminder of the purpose for which He established the family in the world.... In the Message of Fatima, God calls on us to turn our eyes to the Holy Family of Nazareth, into which He chose to be born, and to grow in grace and stature, in order to present to us a model to imitate, as our footsteps tread the path of our pilgrimage to heaven.[33]

The Rosary. At Fatima, Mary asked that we pray the Rosary *daily and properly*, that is, while meditating on the mysteries of Christ. Our Lady told the children on October 13, "Continue to say the Rosary every day." It is not surprising that the Blessed Mother would be so insistent on praying the Rosary, for it has been one of the most powerful prayers throughout history. Many battles, both spiritual and physical, have been won by praying the Rosary. More than ever today's world needs the power of the Rosary. Saint Padre Pio often advocated the Rosary as *the* weapon for our times.

In the Portuguese language, two words are used to refer to the Rosary: one word is used for praying one set of five decades, and Mary used this word when she asked that the Rosary be prayed daily. Another word, "*Rosario,*" includes all twenty of the mysteries (Joyful, Sorrowful, Glorious, and now Luminous). This is the word Mary used when she gave herself the title "The Lady of the Rosary." She is the lady of all the mysteries. Pope Benedict XV, who reigned from 1914 to 1922, said that when we meditate on the mysteries of the Rosary, we are meditating on the chief mysteries of our salvation. So, when Mary said, "I am the Lady of the Rosary," it is as if she said, "I am the Lady of the chief mysteries of Jesus Christ."

The Blessed Mother also tied together the Rosary and the Eucharist in a deep way through her words at Fatima. The chief mysteries of Jesus Christ are celebrated — even made present — in the Holy Eucharist. As the Mother of Jesus Christ and of the Church, Mary is the Mother of these mysteries. She asked that a chapel be built at Fatima, which would both house Our Lord in the Holy Eucharist and honor her as Lady of the Rosary.

Consecration to the Immaculate Heart of Mary. Devotion to the Immaculate Heart of Mary is a way to embrace the totality of the Catholic faith and the practice of the Christian virtues. In the June apparition, Our Lady had told Lucia that she would be left in the world for many years to help "establish in the world devotion to my Immaculate Heart."

At Fatima, Our Lady encouraged many devotions, asking the faithful to pray the Rosary daily and commending the practice of wearing the brown scapular. She also encouraged the faithful to go to sacramental Confession, receive Communion, pray the Rosary, and meditate on the mysteries for fifteen minutes on the first Saturday of five consecutive months when possible. We can choose to live our faith in union with the Immaculate Heart of the Mother of God. When we put these things into practice, Mary becomes an active participant in our spiritual lives and brings us closer to her Son, Jesus.

Changes after the Miracle of the Sun

After the Miracle of the Sun took place on October 13, 1917, many things began to happen in Fatima. Responding to the request of Our Lady to build a chapel, the community started to construct a little chapel at the location of the actual apparition. Many people continued to visit the place of the apparitions, and devotion to Our Lady of Fatima spread.

Meanwhile, worldwide events proved just how important the message of Fatima was. On October 26, 1917, Nicolai Lenin stated, "Our revolution is international and our first enemy is religion." The prophecy of Our Lady about Russia was starting to materialize, for she had warned that if her request to consecrate the country to her Immaculate Heart was not honored, the errors of Russia would spread to all nations. On March 25, 1984, sixty-seven years after the apparitions at Fatima, Pope John Paul II consecrated the entire world to the Immaculate Heart. This act proved to be the beginning of the end of atheistic communism in Russia. We will explore this in more detail in a later chapter.

The Basilica of Our Lady of the Rosary in Fatima was consecrated in 1953, twenty-three years after the Church declared the visions of the three little shepherd children to be "worthy of belief." A second basilica was dedicated in 2007, built to accommodate the millions of people who come to Fatima each year to pray the Rosary and offer petitions to Our Lady.

Fatima the place and Fatima the message both welcome the pilgrim to a place of peace. It is a place of spiritual renewal for those who seek God. As late as 2005, Lucia would express frustration that the true message of Fatima was being ignored and that people dwelled too much on the miracles and secrets and did not live the message in their daily lives. Lucia said, "Do whatever God tells you. That is what Our Lady wants."[34]

The October apparition and final miracle at Fatima are examples of how powerful God really is and how this same power can carry over in our lives if we give ourselves to Him. The message of Fatima reminds us that we are not powerless before the forces of evil. Ultimately, Fatima is nothing less than an invitation to heaven. In order for heaven to take root in our lives, however, we must continue on our paths of conversion and accept the grace God has offered us through Mary.

CHAPTER 4

FRANCISCO AND THE HIDDEN JESUS

Since Our Lady appeared at Fatima in 1917, much has been written about the three seers, but very little of it has been focused on Francisco. Francisco has often been looked upon as the least favored of the three little shepherds, perhaps because he only saw Our Lady, and neither heard nor spoke to her.

Francisco was born to Manuel and Olimpia de Jesus Marto on June 11, 1908. He was nine years old at the time of the apparitions. During the appearances of the Angel and of the Blessed Virgin, he saw all, but he did not hear the words that were spoken, and had to rely on Lucia and Jacinta's reports afterward. Those who study the message of Fatima often ask why Francisco was unable to hear the words of Our Lady. Perhaps there is room for self-examination here, for how often do we fail to hear Our Lord and Our Lady in our lives? In that way, we are not so different from Francisco.

In his book *The Message of Fatima*, Father C. C. Martindale, S.J., describes Francisco as a sturdy little boy with a round face, small mouth, and a well-formed chin. He liked to hunt snakes, lizards, and moles, alarming his mother when he brought them back home. Everyone found him easygoing, not caring too much about anything. He loved flowers and the effects of light, especially at sunrise and sunset. His favorite pastime was playing the flute. He imitated birds but would never take them from their nests. He once ran all the way home to collect the equivalent of two pennies to persuade another boy to release a bird he had caught. A sensitive child, when preparing for his first Holy Communion, he got muddled in reciting the Creed and was sent home in tears by the priest. Ti Marto, Francisco's father, described him as gentle by nature, affectionate, and seldom disruptive of the family peace.

Here is what Lucia said of Francisco:

> In our games he was quite lively; but few of us liked to play with him as he nearly always lost. I must confess that I myself did not always feel too kindly disposed towards him, as his naturally calm temperament exasperated my own excessive vivacity. Sometimes, I caught him by the arm, made him sit down on the ground or on a stone, and told him to keep still; he obeyed me as if I had real authority over him. Afterwards, I felt sorry, and went and took him by the hand, and he would come along with me as good humouredly as though nothing had happened.[35]

After the apparitions, Lucia had to explain to Francisco many times what the Angel and Our Lady had said. At the first apparition of the Angel, she had to explain to him the meaning of the word "almighty" and also what the Angel had meant when he had said: "The hearts of Jesus and Mary are attentive to the voice of your supplications."

At the Angel's third appearance, when the children received Holy Communion, Lucia was given the Sacred Host and Francisco and Jacinta the chalice. After this apparition, Francisco began questioning again: "Oh, Lucia, the Angel gave you Holy Communion, but what was it he gave to Jacinta and me?" Francisco was accustomed to seeing people at Mass receive the Host but not the chalice. It was Jacinta who answered his question: "Didn't you see that it was the blood that fell from the host?" This supernatural gift left Francisco in deep contemplation at the time, and he said, "I felt that God was in me, and I did not understand in what way."[36]

Francisco's unique spirituality made him more engaged with consoling Our Lord than converting sinners. Thus, he was a great promoter of reparation. In Lucia's memoirs, she illustrated Francisco's desires: "One day I asked him: 'Francisco, which do you like best: to console Our Lord or to convert sinners so as to prevent souls from going to hell?'" Francisco responded to Lucia: "I liked more to console Our Lord. Didn't you notice last month how Our Lady was so sad when She said people must no longer offend God, Our Lord, who is already much offended? I wanted to console Our Lord and, afterward, to convert sinners so they will no longer offend Him."[37]

The priority of consoling God was so clear in his mind that he would speak of it quite often. Sister Lucia told of one day when she was visiting Francisco, already in his final sickness, and he complained about a massive headache. When Jacinta reminded him to offer it up for the conversion of sinners, he replied: "Yes, but first I offer it to console Our Lord and Our Lady; and only then I offer it for sinners and for the Holy Father."[38]

Father Alonso, in his little-known posthumous work *Doctrina y espiritualidad del mensaje de Fatima*, stated that Francisco possessed a mystical perception of the highest level, so that even the vision of hell did not make as strong an impression on him because he saw the mystery of evil and sin in the superior light of mystical contemplation. Father Alonso also explains that this mystical side of Francisco was only satisfied by what the children used to call the "reflex," a phenomenon whereby the visionaries would see themselves as if they were submerged in God.

Sister Lucia further explained: "What most impressed or absorbed [Francisco] was God, the Blessed Trinity, in that immense light that penetrated even into the most intimate recesses of our souls."[39]

Throughout the apparitions, Francisco never saw himself as having been granted less than the other seers. He always wanted to know what it was that the Lady had said, but was equally eager to speak of the wonders he had seen and felt. "We were on fire, in that light which is God," he commented to the other two, "and we didn't burn up! What God is like! We can't speak of it. Yes, about that we can never speak. But, how awful that He is so sad! If only I could comfort Him."[40]

Francisco had a contemplative nature. He had to think, inquire, and then pray. When Lucia asked Our Lady if Francisco would go to heaven, Our Lady said, "Yes, but first he must say many Rosaries." After learning about this from Lucia, Francisco cried out excitedly: "Oh, Our Lady, I will say all the Rosaries you wish!"[41]

When Francisco's brother John Marto was interviewed in later years, he was asked if he thought Francisco was holier than himself when he was a boy. John answered, "No, not until I noticed he was always saying the Rosary. At this point I would go and hide from him so I didn't have to see him always praying that Rosary." Many times, when Lucia and Jacinta would ask Francisco to play, he would immediately hold up his rosary beads.

Francisco's insistence on praying the Rosary shows us even today the power this prayer has to affect our lives and help us to obtain holiness.[42]

We are indebted to Lucia for writing about Francisco exactly as she remembered him. From her accounts, we know that the three children experienced the Fatima apparitions in ways infinitely more complex than mere sight or words alone. Those who questioned the children wanted to know what the Lady looked like and what she said, not suspecting that the answers they received were small parts of the whole experience. Francisco never felt that any privileges had been withheld from him. Instead, he knew he had received a great deal upon which to meditate, as he prayed and made sacrifices for Our Lord.

On August 13, 1917, at the young age of nine, Francisco found himself abducted along with his sister and cousin. The county administrator could think of no better way to unmask what he believed to be a clerical conspiracy to exploit gullible peasants than to lock up the seers. Part of the time, the three children were held in a dark room by themselves, but the rest of the time they were kept in the local jail with adult prisoners. The administrator's superiors expected him to get to the bottom of this so-called scandal that had erupted and was making embarrassing national headlines.

Throughout the forty-eight-hour ordeal, Francisco never cried, but comforted the girls. In jail, he took a medal he wore around his neck, hung it on the wall, and started praying the Rosary. Some of the prisoners knelt and joined in. Seeing that one of them had kept his head covered, Francisco scolded him. The man immediately handed his cap to Francisco, who placed it on a windowsill on top of his own. When he saw Jacinta being taken away — supposedly to be boiled alive — he uncovered his head to say a Hail Mary. "What are you up to?" asked one of the guards. "Praying so that Jacinta won't be afraid," answered Francisco. He was a tough boy; men had no power to intimidate him. He waited calmly to die for the truth that he had seen the Lady. In the end, his courageous faith posed an insurmountable obstacle to any claims that Fatima had been concocted, rehearsed, and staged by the clergy.

Nearly all who held power in 1917 Portugal were Freemasons. It is not surprising that the Masons took such an interest in opposing the appearances at Fatima, for the rapidly spreading story of the apparitions challenged their great power in the country. To combat the influence of Fatima, the Masons abused the clergy in the press. They sent troops to disturb the crowds drawn to Fatima by word of mouth. They even exploded dynamite at the site of the apparitions. Yet despite all of their efforts, they were unable to explain why the children spoke of different experiences of the apparitions, especially Francisco claiming not to be able to hear the Lady. The testimonies the three simple little shepherds held, even in the face of death threats, foiled the secular state's attempt at building a case against the clergy.

Finally, on August 15, the authorities released the children. "All these things happen by the power from on high," exclaimed Ti Marto, upon recovering his children. Local men, armed with all kinds of implements, stood ready to settle accounts with the government official. Mr. Marto understood well that the Masons' extreme behavior had merely served to confirm the truth of what the children had been saying.

If either of the Marto parents doubted something supernatural and holy was indeed taking place, they had only to observe the quiet transformation occurring in their two youngest children. The change was unmistakable, even though the children tried to hide it. One night, Ti Marto awoke to the sounds of sobbing coming from Francisco's room. He tiptoed across the house, oil lamp in hand, and found his son with his head buried in his pillow, trying to muffle his crying. Asked if he was in pain, Francisco answered that he was crying because "God is so sad, on account of so many sins that people commit all the time." Ti Marto reflected later: "I felt myself seized by a great respect for my son, and realized how great is the power of God!" It was obvious to him that great things were going on with his children. Though young and uneducated, Francisco had been granted an understanding of sin and of the effects of sin. He expressed that understanding in terms of the sadness of God, and always in the present tense: "God is so sad."[43]

Comforting God for the sadness caused Him by sin became Francisco's very special area of spiritual endeavor. During the year following the apparitions, whenever he accompanied Jacinta and Lucia to school, he often told them as they passed the church: "You go on. I'll stay here with the Hidden Jesus. I don't need to learn how to read because I'm going to heaven soon. Come and get me after school."[44] Knowing that he would not be on earth much longer, Francisco decided to spend the time he had left in prayer. The parish church was undergoing renovation at the time, and the Blessed Sacrament was on a temporary altar behind the baptismal font. Francisco would squeeze in between and remain all day next to the tabernacle, lost in prayer, comforting

God. He did this even after he became ill, as long as he could drag his little feet.

The mystical quality of Francisco's prayer life is not for us to know. But one particular incident, recorded by Lucia, shows how deeply he communicated with Jesus in the Sacred Host. The three were on the way to school one morning when Lucia's married sister met them on the road to tell them of a village boy who had been arrested, falsely accused of a crime that carried a long prison sentence. The boy's mother was in great affliction and wished them to pray for her son. As they passed by the church, Francisco told Lucia and Jacinta: "While you go to school, I'll stay with the Hidden Jesus. I'll ask Him for that favor."[45]

After school, Lucia went to the church to get Francisco. "Did you ask Jesus for that favor?"

"Yes. Tell your sister that the boy will be back home in a few days." And he was, wrote Lucia.[46]

On December 23, 1918, Francisco developed bronchial pneumonia. He said, "I will go to heaven soon and when I am there I will be able to console Our Lord and Our Lady a great deal." One morning, one of his older sisters knocked at the door of Lucia's home. Francisco had taken a turn for the worse and was asking to see her. Lucia entered Francisco's room, and the two were left alone. Many people reported feeling as if they were in the presence of God when they came near him, especially in these last days. "I'm going to make my Confession, in order to receive Communion and die," Francisco told her. "I want you to tell me whether you saw me commit any sins, and then go and ask Jacinta if she saw me commit any."

"You disobeyed your mother sometimes," Lucia told him, "when she told you to stay home and you left the house."

"It's true, I have that one. Now go and ask Jacinta if she can remember any others."[47]

Lucia went to Jacinta's bedside to do as he asked. She returned with Jacinta's report: "Once, before Our Lady came, you stole a tostão [a coin worth 10–25 cents] from your father, to buy a harmonica.... And one time you joined in when boys were throwing stones at each other."

"I already confessed those," Francisco replied. "But I will confess them again. Perhaps it's because of those sins I committed that Our Lord is so sad. But even if I weren't to die, I would never commit them again. I am sorry now."[48]

The priest came to Francisco's room that day to hear his Confession, and brought him Communion the following day. After receiving the Hidden Jesus, he lay for a long time with his eyes shut, filled with gratitude. "Today," he said to Jacinta, "I am happier than you are, for I have the Hidden Jesus in my heart!"[49]

Francisco's witness challenges us all. How do we respond when we receive Jesus in the Holy Eucharist? Is it simply out of habit, or with profound love? Often, in the rush of our everyday lives, we lose focus on our spiritual lives. Francisco grew in faith through what became a life of constant prayer, especially praying the Rosary.

The evening before Francisco died, Lucia came to see him for a final farewell. She said, "Goodbye, Francisco. If you die during the night, do not forget me up there!"

Francisco replied, "You may rest assured, I will never forget you," and he took her hand and gazed at her for a long time as tears welled in his eyes.

As Lucia left she told him, "Goodbye then, Francisco, until we meet in heaven."[50]

On April 4, 1919, Francisco saw a shining light by the door. Olimpia Marto later remembered only that her son Francisco had quietly announced the appearance of light by the door, and died happily. Francisco's last few words confirmed what he had been saying for the prior two years — that Our Lady would come soon to take him to heaven.

Next to the room where the boy smiled his last lay Jacinta, also sick, needing care as she awaited her turn to be taken to heaven by Our Lady. Grief filled the Marto household, yet there was also an abundance of grace and quiet heroism. The Martos knew that God was near in these final days.

Francisco teaches us the power of praying the Rosary and the awesomeness of Jesus in the Holy Eucharist. In Francisco, we also see the powerful faith of ordinary children. As Jesus says, "Unless you turn and become like children, you will not enter the kingdom of heaven" (Mt 18:3). What faith, what love, what depths even children are capable of in the spiritual life! We must never fail to offer children the fullness of true faith, trusting the Holy Spirit to work in their tender souls.

CHAPTER 5

JACINTA:
PROPHET AND MYSTIC

Despite her youth, she had a great understanding of the mysteries of faith, and she lived in deep union with God. Jacinta was truly a prophet and mystic. Her life stands as a poignant reminder that God uses even humble children to deliver a powerful message to the world.

It was Sister Lucia who gave the Church a greater understanding of Jacinta's mission. Lucia once commented that when souls are given special revelations from heaven, they are also given lights to comprehend the message, and that this was especially true of Jacinta. "Jacinta seemed to have this discernment to an extremely high degree," Lucia said. "Jacinta was the one who received from Our Lady a greater abundance of grace, and a better knowledge of God and of virtue."[51]

Jacinta, small as she was, possessed a deep spirit of sacrifice and penance, and she had a keen understanding of suffering. When asked about this in later years, Sister Lucia answered:

> I think the reason is this: firstly, God willed to bestow on her a special grace, through the Immaculate Heart of Mary; and secondly, it was because she had looked upon hell, and had seen the ruin of souls who fall therein. Some people, even the most devout, refuse to speak to children about hell, in case it would frighten them. Yet God did not hesitate to show hell to three children, one of

whom was only six years old, knowing well that they would be horrified to the point of, I would almost dare to say, withering away with fear. Jacinta often sat thoughtfully on the ground or on a rock, and exclaimed: "Oh, hell! hell! How sorry I am for the souls who go to hell! And the people down there, burning alive, like wood in the fire!" Then, shuddering, she knelt down with her hands joined, and recited the prayer that Our Lady had taught us: "O my Jesus, forgive us; save us from the fire of hell; take all souls to Heaven, especially those most in need."[52]

A great transformation came over Jacinta following the apparitions, a transformation that grew with each appearance of the Blessed Mother and reached a climax during the last part of her life. Jacinta loved singing and dancing. She loved flowers and always gathered a bouquet of wild flowers whenever she went to the Cabeço. She would give these flowers to Lucia or strew them over her like the flower petals that were often scattered before the Most Blessed Sacrament in processions.

After Our Lady first appeared, Lucia made her cousins promise to keep the visit a secret. Jacinta promised not to utter a word, but she could not contain herself. Something inside her just made her tell her parents, and the news quickly spread throughout the village of Aljustrel and, from there, all over Portugal and throughout the world. Lucia and Francisco scolded her for blurting out their secret, and Jacinta suffered greatly at this. In the end, however, her inability to keep the Lady's visits a secret proved providential.

Jacinta the Prophet

Jacinta developed a great devotion to the Holy Father. She added three Hail Marys to her Rosary for him. Sister Lucia wrote of a time when the children were taking their siesta down by her parents' well. Jacinta called out to Lucia: "Didn't you see the Holy Father?"

"No."

"I don't know how it was, but I saw the Holy Father in a very big house, kneeling by a table, with his head buried in his hands, and he was weeping. Outside the house, there were many people. Some of them were throwing stones. Others were cursing him and using bad language. Poor Holy Father, we must pray very much for him."[53]

Sister Lucia recalled another time when two priests urged the children to pray for the Holy Father. "Is he the one I saw weeping, the one Our Lady told us about in the secret?" Jacinta asked.

"Yes, he is," Lucia answered.[54]

Jacinta became ill in October 1918, during a significant epidemic of influenza. She contracted bronchial pneumonia and developed purulent pleurisy, which caused her great pain. Shortly before this, Francisco had come down with influenza, which took his life in April 1919. Jacinta tried to hide her intense sufferings from her mother, and would tell her, "Don't worry, Mother, I am going to Heaven and I shall pray for you very much. Don't cry, because I'm all right." She did admit her suffering to Lucia, however, relating that she was offering it all for the conversion of sinners. Then she would say: "Don't tell anyone how much I suffer, especially Mother. I don't want her to worry."[55]

Jacinta's illness reduced her from exuberant health and spirits to little more than a skeleton. Still, she would struggle out of bed to bow her head to the floor when praying, especially the act of adoration taught the children by the Angel. She thought of others, not herself, even in her extreme illness.

In July 1919, Jacinta's father placed his sick daughter upon the wagon, and they set off for Saint Augustine's Hospital in Vila Nova de Ourém. It was a difficult journey for Jacinta. Likewise, the two months at Saint Augustine's Hospital were painful. But Jacinta was relieved on two different occasions when her cousin Lucia came to visit her. During one of these visits,

> Jacinta told Lucia that she was suffering a lot but that she was offering everything for sinners and in reparation to the immaculate heart of Mary. "Oh how much I love to suffer for the love of them (Jesus and Mary), just to give them pleasure. They greatly love those who suffer for the conversion of sinners."[56]

Jacinta had been getting out of bed to say the prayer of the Angel, but she kept falling because she could not get her head to the floor any longer. She was therefore reduced to saying it on her knees.

Jacinta is a powerful example of what it means to offer daily sacrifices to God. Do we turn our daily discomforts, irritations, and sufferings into opportunities to love God and others more? Or do we rely on the comforts of life? What would happen to us, and to our faith, if we had to give any of them up?

One of the most profound examples of Jacinta's sanctification was her devotion to the Eucharist. Jacinta would ask: "Lucia, have you been to Holy Communion today? Then come close to me because you have the hidden Jesus in your heart." She would also say: "I don't know how it is, but I feel Our Lord inside me and I understand what He says though I can't see Him and hear Him, but I love to be with Him." She called Jesus in the Most Blessed Sacrament "the hidden Jesus." When Lucia showed Jacinta a picture of a chalice and Host, Jacinta kissed it, saying: "It's the hidden Jesus; how I love Him. If only I could receive Him in the church. Can you go to Holy Communion in Heaven? If so, I shall go every day. If the Angel could go to the hospital and take me Holy Communion how happy I should be."[57]

Despite her illness, Jacinta was a missionary as well as a mystic. Confined to her bed after returning from a lengthy hospital stay, Jacinta would teach the neighbor children to say the Our Father and the Hail Mary, to bless themselves, or to sing hymns. She would also say the Rosary with them and warn them not to offend God or they might go to hell.

As can best be determined, it was sometime near the end of December 1919 when Our Lady appeared to Jacinta again to tell her that she would soon be taken to heaven from a hospital in faraway Lisbon. This is how Jacinta related it to Lucia: "She told me that I am going to Lisbon to another hospital, that I will not see you again, nor my parents either, and after suffering a great deal I shall die alone. But she said I must not be afraid, since she herself is coming to take me to Heaven." In tears, Jacinta threw her arms around Lucia. "I will never see you again! You won't be coming to visit me there. Oh please pray hard for me because I am going to die alone."[58]

Other bits of conversations reveal the feelings in Jacinta's heart. One day Lucia found her kissing a picture of Mary and saying, "Darling Mother in Heaven, must I die alone?"

Attempting to comfort her, Lucia said: "What does it matter if you die alone, if Our Lady is coming to fetch you?"

Lucia wrote that the separation from Jacinta was heartbreaking. "She stayed a long time in my arms and then said, sobbing, 'We shall never see each other again! But pray for me very much until I go to Heaven and then I will pray very much for you. Don't ever tell the secret to anyone even if they kill you. Love Jesus very much and the Immaculate Heart, and make many sacrifices for sinners.'"

In Lisbon, Jacinta and her mother, Senhora Marto, were first taken in by a nun named Mother Godinho, who ran an orphanage. How delighted Jacinta was to discover that at the orphanage she was under the same roof that housed a chapel of Our Lady of the Holy Miracles, where the hidden Jesus was present in the tabernacle. In addition to access to a chapel for adoration, Jacinta was close to other sacraments while in Lisbon. One day Jacinta said, "Oh Mother, I want to go to Confession." They went to the basilica, and when Jacinta came out of the confessional she said to her mother, "What a good priest that was. He asked me so many things!"

But while she had the blessings of the sacraments and Mother Godinho at the orphanage, Jacinta was not to have the comforts of family for long. Senhora Marto was anxious to return to Aljustrel where she was needed to care for her eldest daughter, Florinda, who was also seriously ill. Jacinta did not cry when her mother took leave for Aljustrel. She knew from Our Lady that it was God's will that she must die without any of her family or relatives at her side. She embraced her mother bravely and said, "Good-bye, Mother, until we meet in Heaven."

Mother Godinho carefully recorded the following words on various subjects spoken by Jacinta:

> Regarding sin: The sins which cause most souls to go to hell are the sins of the flesh. Fashions will much offend Our Lord. People who serve God should not follow the fashions. The Church has no fashions. Our Lord is always the same. The sins of the world are very great. If men knew what eternity is they would do everything to change their lives. People are lost because they do not think of the death of Our Lord and do not do penance. Many marriages are not of God and do not please Our Lord.
>
> Regarding war: Our Lady said that the world is full of war and discords. Wars are the punishments for sin. Our Lady cannot at present avert the justice of her Son from the world. Penance is necessary. If people amend their lives, Our Lord will even yet save the world, but if not, punishment will come.
>
> Regarding priests, religious, and rulers: You must pray much for sinners and for priests and religious. Priests should concern themselves only with the things of the Church. Priests must be very, very pure. Disobedience of priests and religious to their superiors displeases Our Lord very much. Pray, mother, for rulers. Heaven forgive those who persecute the Church of Christ. If the government

would leave the Church in peace and give liberty to religion it would have God's blessing.

Regarding the virtues: Have charity even for bad people. Do not speak evil of people and fly from those who do. Sacrifice pleases Our Lord very much. Confession is a sacrament of mercy and we must confess with joy and trust. There can be no salvation without Confession. The Mother of God wants more virgin souls bound by a vow of chastity. I would gladly go to a convent but I would rather go to Heaven. To be a religious one must be very pure in body and mind.[59]

One day Mother Godinho asked Jacinta: "Do you know what it means to be pure?"

Jacinta answered: "Yes, yes, I know. To be pure in body means to be chaste, and to be pure in mind means not to commit sins; not to look at what one should not see, not to steal or lie and always to speak the truth even if it is hard." It is to be noted that Jacinta more than once related Our Lady's words about impurity. Sehnora Marto recalls that Jacinta once said, "Mother, you must never eat flesh [meat] on Fridays, nor give it to us because Our Lady said that sins of the flesh brought people to hell." She also stated: "Doctors do not know how to cure people properly because they do not have the love of God."

Mother Godinho asked, "Who taught you these things?"

Jacinta answered, "Our Lady, but some of them I thought myself."[60]

Mother Godinho spoke with Jacinta's mother before she had to return to Aljustrel. In addition to Jacinta, Sehnora Marta had two other daughters, Florinda and Teresa, and when Mother Godinho asked her if she would like these two daughters to enter the religious life, the woman expressed her natural reaction: "Heavens, no!" Jacinta had not heard this, but shortly thereafter she said to Mother Godinho, "Our Lady would like my sisters to be nuns although mother wouldn't like it, and so she will take them to Heaven before long." The two daughters died shortly after Jacinta's death, at the ages of seventeen and sixteen.

Jacinta even predicted that one day Mother Godinho would visit the Cova da Iria, but that this would take place after Jacinta's death. The nun had a great desire to visit the Cova because she believed the Mother of God had appeared there. As we shall see later, circumstances kept Jacinta's body from being buried in Lisbon as first intended, and Mother Godinho was chosen to accompany it to the family vault of Baron Alvaiazere in Vila Nova de Ourém; thus she was able to visit Fatima and the Cova da Iria.

Jacinta the Mystic

Jacinta came to love the orphanage and Mother Godinho, but God would require still another sacrifice of her. Mother Godinho received serious reprimands from both doctors and nurses when they learned that she had accepted a tuberculous patient into the orphanage. They considered this a serious risk of infection for the other children. Mother Godinho had taken Jacinta in out of charity, since the people who had originally agreed to house her when she arrived in Lisbon had refused to do so after seeing how sick she was. Mother Godinho's charity certainly blessed the Church today. We have her notes to thank for the insights into the mystical experiences of a child who reached great sanctity before the age of ten.

Sister Lucia never knew Mother Godinho, yet the writings of Mother Godinho and those of Sister Lucia about Jacinta are in striking agreement concerning the child's profound spirituality. One time Jacinta asked the nun to go to the chapel to make reparation to Our Lord. "Look, go to the Tabernacle with another nun, and kneel at each side of it, and pray as the angels do in Heaven."

Mother Godinho asked Jacinta, "Have you ever seen the angels adore Jesus?"

Jacinta answered that she had heard them sing, but that it was not the way the people sang. Jacinta would remain silent for hours, and when asked what she had been thinking about, she would usually reply that it had been about Our Lady, who was so beautiful, or else about heaven.

At the insistence of the medical professionals, and to the disappointment of Jacinta and Mother Godinho, Jacinta was transferred to the hospital on February 2, 1920. Her surroundings there were cold and lonely. She suffered from the overly decorative dress of visitors and nurses, whose clothing Jacinta considered immodest. Of doctors who were unbelievers she said, "Poor things! If they knew what awaited them!" Jacinta revealed that Our Lady appeared to her at the hospital again and spoke of the many sins of luxury and of the flesh, sins which were causing so many souls to be lost. Our Lady spoke of the necessity of penance for these sins.

Jacinta had brief moments of joy when special visitors came. Her father, Ti Marto, came once. He could stay but a very short time, for he had to return promptly to his other sick children in Aljustrel.

The doctors planned an operation, which they thought might save Jacinta's life. Jacinta dictated a letter about this to be sent to Lucia. (Sister Lucia could not recall whether or not she had received such a letter.) She wrote that the operation would not help, for Our Lady had appeared to her and revealed the day and hour of her death. No one ever heard her complain. Rather, she said, "We must suffer if we want to go to Heaven." Our Lady did not neglect her specially favored soul during the time at the hospital. Mother Godinho received the confidences of Jacinta, who told the nun that the Blessed Virgin Mary would occasionally appear to her. During the last days before her death, Jacinta said, "Now I'm much better. Our Lady said that she would soon come to fetch me and that she would take away the pain."

One of the doctors who treated Jacinta, Dr. Lisboa, was greatly impressed with the girl. He clearly recalled:

> And in fact, with the apparition, there in the middle of the ward, her pain completely disappeared and she began to be able to play and enjoy certain distractions. She liked to look at holy pictures, one among them in particular — given me later as a souvenir — of Our Lady of Sameiro which she said most closely resembled the Lady of the apparitions. I was told several times that Jacinta wished to see me, but as my professional duties were heavy and Jacinta was apparently better I, unfortunately, put off my visit until too late.[61]

Mother Godinho would visit Jacinta at the hospital. When she sat at the patient's bedside in the place where God's Mother appeared, Jacinta would object: "Not there, Mother, that's where Our Lady stood." On one occasion, one of the nurses purposely stood in that place, as Jacinta constantly looked toward that spot. The nurse related: "She did not say anything but her face took on such an expression of pain that I felt I could not remain there."

At one point Our Lady offered Jacinta a choice. She could die earlier and go to heaven right away, or live longer in order to be able to offer up more suffering in reparation and for the conversion of poor sinners. Jacinta chose to stay longer to help save more souls. A few days after the operation, Mother Godinho asked the doctor's permission to move Jacinta back to the orphanage, since Jacinta also desired this. The doctor responded that it would risk her life, so the request was dropped. On February 17, Jacinta saw Our Lady, who told her that she would soon come to fetch her and take away her pain. It was also at this time that Our Lady gave some important communications, which Jacinta related to Mother Godinho. Among them was that impurity was the sin that sent most people to perdition; that people should not remain obstinate in their sins as they had done up until then; that it was necessary to do much penance; and that people should do without luxuries.

About this last apparition of Our Lady to Jacinta, Lucia wrote: "I have frequently been asked if Our Lady has pointed out in some apparition the kind of sin that displeased Our Lord the most, owing to Jacinta's having mentioned the sin of the flesh in Lisbon. I think now that she must have put the same question to Our Lady as she had done to me, and obtained the answer from her."

Jacinta stated that Our Lady had repeated her declaration that she would appear a seventh time. The little girl commented that it would not be to her, as she was going to die. She added that Our Lady wore a very sad expression on her face when speaking. The young mystic said, "I am so sorry for Our Lady! I am so sorry for her!"[62]

A study of the sayings of Jacinta brings to light the mystical gifts which were so evident in Lisbon. Even before going there, she had been transformed from a sweet and carefree child into a girl still tender and loving, but also serious. She possessed a spiritual insight like that of some of the Church's great saints who reached such heights only when much older. We can see evidence of the serious relationship Jacinta had with God in these words: "I love to tell Jesus that I love Him. When I say it often, it seems to me that I have a flame in my heart, but one which does not burn me. I can never get tired of telling Our Lord and Our Lady that I love them so much."[63]

Shortly before going to Lisbon, Jacinta said to Lucia:

> It will not be long now before I go to Heaven. You will remain here to announce that God wishes devotion to the Immaculate Heart to be established in the world. When you go to say that, do not hide yourself; tell everybody that God concedes us His graces through the Immaculate Heart of Mary; that people should invoke her; that the Heart of Jesus wishes the Heart of Mary to be venerated at His side. Let them ask for peace through the Immaculate Heart of Mary, for God has given it to her. Ah, if I could only put into people's hearts the flame that is burning within my own heart, and that is making me love the Hearts of Jesus and Mary so much![64]

Jacinta said that sinners deeply offended the Divine Heart of Our Lord. If they would amend their lives, He would help them. If not, they would suffer a punishment such as had never been experienced at any time. She condemned riches, except when used to good purpose. She saw wars as punishments for sins. With her eyes lowered and her hands clasped, Jacinta would often murmur, "Oh, hell! Oh, hell! Mother of God, have pity on me and on sinners!" The vision of hell was not revealed to the world until years later, when Sister Lucia was told in prayer that it was time to reveal the first two parts of the secret: the vision of hell and devotion to the Immaculate Heart of Mary. For this reason, Jacinta's frequent references to hell were mostly lost upon those at the orphanage who heard them.

Jacinta's great love for Jesus in Holy Communion was revealed on numerous occasions. She had received her first Holy Communion from the Angel years before. Afterward, she longed for the Angel to bring her Holy Communion again, saying that if one could receive Communion in heaven, she intended to receive Our Lord there every day. There were times when she would cry out: "Am I going to die without receiving the hidden Jesus? If only Our Lady would bring Him to me when she comes to fetch me!"[65]

Jacinta commented to Lucia that she was so sorry not to be able to go to Holy Communion in reparation for the sins committed against the Immaculate Heart of Mary. Jacinta's desire for the Holy Eucharist, however, was granted when she reached Lisbon. Her spiritual maturity was evident in her deep devotion to this central mystery of our Faith, the mystery in which the perfect offering and reparation of Jesus are given to the Blessed Trinity.

Jacinta died peacefully at 10:30 p.m. on February 20, 1920. Dr. Lisboa reported Jacinta's death as follows:

On the evening of the 20th of February, at about 6 o'clock, Jacinta said that she felt worse and wished to receive the Sacraments. The parish priest [Dr. Pereira do Reis] was called and he heard her Confession about 8 o'clock that night. I was told that Jacinta had insisted that the Blessed Sacrament be brought to her as Viaticum but that Dr. Reis had not concurred because she seemed fairly well. He promised to bring her Holy Communion in the morning. Jacinta again asked for Viaticum saying that she would shortly die, and indeed, she died that night. Jacinta died peacefully at 10:30 p.m., peacefully, but without having received Holy Communion.

Senhor Almeida, who assisted at the undertaking procedures, later wrote:

I seem to see Jacinta still, looking like a little angel. In her coffin she seemed to be alive; her lips and checks were a beautiful pink. I have seen many corpses, large and small, but I have never seen anything like that. The beautiful perfume which the body exhaled could not be explained naturally and the hardest sceptic could not doubt it. One remembers the smell which so often makes it repugnant to remain near a corpse and yet this child had been dead three days and a half and the smell of her body was like a bouquet of flowers.[66]

Fourteen years later, on September 12, 1934, a canonical inquiry into the extraordinary facts of Jacinta's life was made in Leiria. It was then decided to transfer Jacinta's remains from the family vault of the Baron de Alvaiazere in Vila Nova de Ourém to the Fatima cemetery, to be placed in a little tomb over Francisco's grave. Thus, Jacinta's prediction — that she would return to Fatima after her death — was fulfilled one year later, on September 12, 1935, at the order of the bishop of Leiria. The bishop decided to hasten the date for the translation of the body to the basilica at the Cova da Iria, even though construction on the basilica had not yet been completed.

Though her bodily remains were moved in 1935, it was not until much later that her tomb was opened and everything was examined. On the morning of April 30, 1951, the tomb was opened with many witnesses present, including the bishop of Leiria and members of the seers' families. Doctors who were present to examine the remains, along with the workmen, took solemn oaths that they would state the truth and only the truth. The body of Jacinta was easily authenticated. The exposed face was found to be incorrupt, as were the hands. The entire body was not examined. The face looked more worn than it had in the photograph taken at the first exhumation on September 12, 1935.

On May 13, 2000, Pope John Paul II publicly thanked Jacinta for her prayers and sacrifices for the Holy Father. He seemed to sense that the prayers and sacrifices of the three little children — especially Jacinta's — played a role in sparing his life during the attempted assassination of May 13, 1981.

Through the intercession of Saint Jacinta, and by her example, we may come to understand the power of prayer, penance, and sacrifice. That depth of understanding is the key to becoming more willing to offer what we suffer for the salvation of souls.

Chapter 6

Sister Lucia:
Lifetime of Witness

Lucia Dos Santos, the youngest daughter of Antonio and Maria Rosa Dos Santos, was born on Holy Thursday, March 28, 1907, in Aljustrel, Portugal. She was baptized on March 30 in the parish church of Saint Anthony. Lucia was an extroverted child, though not considered a pretty girl.

Lucia remembered much of her happy childhood: "The good Lord deigned to endow me with the use of reason while I was still very much a child. I can remember being aware of my actions while still a baby in my mother's arms. I can remember being rocked to sleep, and at the same time lullabies being sung. On account of housework, I remember my mother handing me to my father, who in turn would shower me with tenderness and affection." As the last of seven children — six girls and one boy — Lucia enjoyed a childhood of caresses and favors.

Lucia shared how she learned to pray and dance:

The first thing I learned was the Hail Mary, for my mother held me constantly in her arms while she was teaching my sister the prayers.

I would tag along with my older sisters to local dances and dances in the parish. At the dances, they would put me on top of a trunk or some other high object so I would not get trampled on by those present. My sisters would teach me the words to the various songs, as well as how to dance some waltzes.[67]

In 1915, Lucia's journey toward the apparitions began. Her mother decided that Lucia was ready to tend and care for the flock of sheep. At first, her father and sisters did not agree because she was so well-loved at home. She would often invite friends from the community to come with her and pray. One day after lunch, Lucia and her friends were praying the Rosary when they saw a figure in the air above the trees. Lucia said, "It looked like a statue made of snow." All of the children present said they saw the figure, and they went home that night and told their families. Lucia did not. Still, her mother heard about it and scolded Lucia, saying that it was just, "childish nonsense." Lucia forgot about this strange apparition and continued with her work.

In 1916, Lucia's cousins Jacinta and Francisco received permission from their parents to take over their own flock, so Lucia left her friends and joined her cousins, thus setting the stage for the apparitions that would soon begin. While they herded the sheep, Lucia would catechize her two younger cousins.

In interviews conducted and published by Father Fox in the *Fatima Family Messenger*, Teresa de Jesus Reis, a childhood friend of Lucia's, offered many details about Lucia as a child. "Lucia was very pleasant and kind. She would bring cornbread for lunch and would share her lunch with others. I remember her sharing lunch one time with me and Maria. Lucia was always very lively. She would make up songs. I remember one time when she made up a song about her sister who was going with a young man. She did this to tease her sister."

She also related how Lucia described the Lady she saw at the Cova: "She said she was white and glowing. Lucia said that always before Our Lady would appear, the atmosphere would get something like a thunderstorm was coming but there was no storm. Even though it was a beautiful day they would hear thunder. Then they'd turn around and see a glow. It was Our Lady of Fatima."

About Lucia's personality even after the apparitions, Teresa said:

> To me she was exactly the same. She was always kind and playful. She still would dance. The Bishop had Lucia removed from this area and taken to the convent because she was so much like the other children. The Bishop wanted to protect her so he did this.
>
> Priests who came to ask questions of the three little shepherds would ask me too. "Did you see her?" I would say "No" because I had not. But something did happen very unusual on May 13, 1917, the day of the miracle when the children saw our Lady. I was not in the Cova. I was near the windmill which was used to make flour. I was herding sheep. Suddenly my sheep were gone. I saw two doves over the Mill. Then in the window of the windmill I saw pure white doves. I had never seen such white doves before. I remember at that time when I was still a child and my friend was with me and this happened with the doves my friend said, "Something new is happening." We did not talk about it anymore and then we heard about the apparitions.
>
> My parents believed in the apparitions from the beginning. At times, I was also in the Cova on

the 13th but the crowd was so big I never even saw Lucia, Jacinta and Francisco there, but then at a later time of the same day, I would see them.[68]

Teresa further recalled "that Lucia was very good, very bright. Lucia, with a lively imagination, could make up songs." Sometimes, Teresa would try to get more information about the apparitions from her friend:

After the apparitions, her family sold all of their sheep. But they kept two goats and sometimes I went with Lucia with her two goats and my sheep. I would say to Lucia, "Tell me the secret. You are my best friend and you don't tell me the secret." Lucia would answer: "Bishops and priests want to know. I won't even tell them." Still I would say, "If you are my best friend you should tell me." Lucia would say, "I can't tell you."[69]

Lucia faced immense pressures after the deaths of Jacinta and Francisco, as people frequently came to Fatima and to her parents' home in Aljustrel pressing for information about the apparitions. The first bishop of the restored Diocese of Leiria was concerned for Lucia and decided that, on June 17, 1921, she should enter the school of the Dorothean Sisters in Vilar without revealing her identity. There she would receive a good moral and religious education. Our Lady had told Lucia to learn how to read and write, so the Bishop was assisting the fulfillment of Our Lady's request

In 1925, at the age of eighteen, Lucia left Vilar to become a postulant in another religious order. She desired to become a Carmelite, but, as she soon learned, our plans do not always match God's design for our lives, at least not immediately. Influenced by the example of her Dorothean instructors, and grateful for her time with them, Lucia chose to enter the institute of Saint Dorothy in Tuy, Spain.

On December 10, 1925, Our Lady appeared to her in the chapel in Tuy with the Child Jesus by her side, elevated on a cloud of light. Our Lady gave her detailed instructions about the acts of reparation to be made on the First Saturdays. Two months later the Child Jesus appeared again to Lucia, asking her if she had begun to spread the First Saturday devotion. Lucia tried to convince Him of the difficulties pointed out by her mother superior and confessor, but he would not accept excuses. The Child Jesus told Lucia, "It is true that your superior alone can do nothing, but with my grace she can do all." After this, Lucia asked a series of questions about the First Saturday devotion, then the Child Jesus disappeared without saying anything more.

It was also while Lucia was in Tuy that Our Lady fulfilled her promise from the Secret of July 13, 1917: "I shall come to ask for the consecration of Russia." Sister Lucia describes the communication, which took place on June 13, 1929:

> I had requested and obtained permission from my superiors and my confessor to make a holy hour from 11:00 p.m. to midnight, from Thursday to Friday of each week.
>
> Finding myself alone one night, I knelt down near the Communion rail, in the middle of the chapel, to recite the prayers of the Angel, lying prostrate.... Feeling tired, I got up and continued

to recite them with my arms in the form of a cross. The only light was that of the [sanctuary] lamp.

Suddenly, the whole chapel lit up with a supernatural light and on the altar appeared a cross of light which reached the ceiling. In a clearer light, on the upper part of the cross, could be seen the face of a man with His body to the waist, on His chest a dove, equally luminous; and nailed to the cross, the body of another man. A little below the waist [of Christ on the cross], suspended in the air, could be seen a Chalice and a large Host, onto which some drops of Blood were falling, which flowed from the face of the Crucified One and from the wound in His breast. Running down over the Host, these drops fell into the Chalice.

Under the right arm of the cross was Our Lady with Her Immaculate Heart in Her hand ... [She appeared as Our Lady of Fatima, with Her Immaculate Heart in Her left hand, without sword or roses, but with a crown of thorns and flames] under the left arm [of the cross], in large letters, like crystalline water which flowed over the altar, forming these words: "Grace and Mercy." I understood that the mystery of the Most Holy Trinity was shown to me, and I received lights about this mystery which I am not permitted to reveal.

Then Our Lady said to me: "The moment has come in which God asks the Holy Father to make, in union with all the bishops of the world, the consecration of Russia to My Immaculate Heart, promising to save it by this means. So numerous are the souls which the justice of God condemns for sins committed against Me, that I come to ask for reparation. Sacrifice yourself for this intention and pray."

I rendered an account of this to my confessor, who ordered me to write down what Our Lord willed to be done.[70]

All the basic doctrines of our faith were contained in this vision: the Blessed Trinity, the Incarnation, and our redemption through the Cross. Specifically, this vision showed how Christ's sacrifice on the cross is made present for us in the Sacrifice of the Mass. It also highlights the role of Mary as the channel of all grace, standing at the foot of the cross, her Immaculate Heart pierced by the sins of humankind. Finally, the vision promotes the Rosary, which, when prayed well, disposes our minds and hearts for fruitful participation in the divine liturgy. If the Church truly practices the Faith as manifested in these mysteries, peace will come to the world, and the present crisis of faith could be overcome. This was the core promise of Fatima, and it is a promise that remains for us. We must continually return to the Immaculate Heart of Mary, calling on her great power and protection.

In particular, the apparition at Tuy clarified the role the bishops, and specifically the Holy Father, were to have in God's plan for peace. At Fatima, the faithful had been instructed in their role of prayer and sacrifice, but at Tuy the pope was given the primary responsibility for future peace.

Sister Lucia remained in the Dorothean institute in Tuy, Spain, until 1946. She returned that year to Fatima to identify the places where the apparitions had occurred. Then, with papal permission, Sister Lucia left the Dorothean Sisters and entered the Carmelite Convent of

Saint Teresa in Coimbra. She made her first profession as a Discalced Carmelite there in 1949.

Lucia presents to us an example of both the active and contemplative life. In a simple yet deep way, she excelled in both during her many years upon earth. Lucia's life shows clearly that the message of Fatima is for all of us. It is not a call to remove ourselves from worldly concerns, but an invitation to be strengthened by daily prayer, the sacramental life, and Eucharistic reparation for the conversion of sinners. This message of Fatima was to be Lucia's mission in the Church and in the world.

Very early on, when Lucia learned that Francisco and Jacinta would die soon, she worried about her mission and the loneliness it would bring. She had asked Our Lady sadly, "Must I stay here alone?" Our Lady responded: "No, my child. And would that make you suffer? Do not be disheartened, I will never leave you. My Immaculate Heart will be your refuge and the way that will lead you to God." We can all take courage and comfort from this promise. All of us are under the care of the Immaculate Heart of Mary and called to carry out the same mission that Lucia was given.

Lucia's desire to promote devotion to Mary was fulfilled behind the cloistered walls of the Carmelite monastery. At Carmel, she was known as Sister Lucia of the Immaculate Heart, a fitting name for her mission on earth. From the cloister, her bishop often gave her permission to write to the Holy Father. The main burden of her mission then was to influence the pope, together with all the Church, to consecrate Russia to the Immaculate Heart of Mary and to make known the devotion of First Saturdays throughout the world. Mary had given this mission to her, a simple girl with the education of a third grader. Once again, Fatima shows us what God can do with the humblest of His people. Lucia certainly was not proud or egotistical about the mission entrusted to her. In fact, the prioress of the Carmelite convent said: "It was not Sister Lucia who wanted to give that message; she was entrusted with giving it to others."[71]

Sister Lucia entered the Discalced Carmelites at the age of forty-one with particular vigor. She fulfilled a variety of offices in the monastery, and the sisters said she performed them excellently. Sister Lucia taught the other sisters how to make rosaries and was a stickler for perfection. One of the sisters stated that she was glad to receive her diploma when she finished making the rosaries. Though some might have thought that her supernatural experiences would have separated her from the daily activities of the monastery, this was not the case. She lived like all of the other sisters in the monastery. As a Carmelite, she lived the rule and sought no dispensation in carrying out what she was asked to do. Under obedience to her superiors, she also carried out correspondence by letters and wrote her memoirs. These writings have become powerful testimony and vehicles of the message of Fatima.

Sister Maria Celina, the prioress of the Coimbra Carmel, "noted Sister Lucia's simplicity, saying that not even the 'burden' of the Fatima secret, which the visionary kept for decades, affected her humility. The prioress, who lived in the same convent with Sister Lucia for twenty-eight years, also recalled the 'normality' of her conversations, adding that the other nuns 'did not ask questions.' The visionary's lack of prominence [in her Carmel community] was such that when Sister Maria Celina first arrived at the Carmel convent, she went 'eight days without knowing that it was

Lucia of Fatima.' With the passing of the years a close bond was established between them, so much so that the prioress said she saw Sister Lucia 'as a niece.'"[72]

It was vital that she integrate into the convent. Sister Lucia had left the Dorotheans in part because too often she was exposed to the public against her own will. She could never live the life of prayer if the Church and her superiors did not hold to rules of seclusion. To enter Carmel is to leave the world for a space and place where one dwells with God alone. That is the vocation of the traditional contemplative Carmelite, and it particularly suited Sister Lucia and her situation. During the many years that she lived in the Carmel at Coimbra, the rule was that, other than cardinals, only relatives or people with special permission from the Vatican could meet with Sister Lucia.

During the months preceding Sister Lucia's death, the convent did not publicize that she was confined to her cell and gradually growing weaker. This silence is understandable, since if the world caught a hint that Sister Lucia could be dying, the convent would have been besieged. The wisdom of the Carmelites was clear, especially in Sister Lucia's dying days.

Despite her continued seclusion from the world, Lucia enjoyed the comforts of her sisters in the convent and the reception of the sacraments. Toward the end of her life, her prioress related, "Age had made her very frail and the doctor advised her not to catch cold, so she heard Mass from her cell and we took her Communion.... In these last days, especially since June 15, one of us was always with her, 24 hours a day. She became much more intimate, from this point of view," which "occurs with all sisters who are dying, because — none has yet died suddenly — when they are in need of our help, there is a greater bond. Since ... her health conditions worsened, she became more dependent on us."[73]

Sister Lucia also received comfort from the pope in her final days. When John Paul II received news that Sister Lucia was ill, he sent her a fax message that was read to her on the eve of her death. Sister Lucia was "deeply moved" by the message from the pope and asked if she could read the fax herself. Even though she was almost blind, she said to her sisters in the community: "Let me read, it's the pope who is writing me." Those present indicated that this was possibly the last reaction she had to life around her. In his message, the Holy Father said that, on hearing of her illness, he prayed to God that she would be able to live "the moment of pain and suffering" with a "paschal spirit," and he ended his message imparting his blessing to her.[74]

Sister Lucia passed away on February 13, 2005 — on the thirteenth day, a date that had become so dear to her. Shortly after the death of Sister Lucia, the prioress stated that Lucia

> was the "jewel" of the Carmelite convent of Coimbra, but within its walls she lived exactly like the other women religious.... The death of the last Fatima seer caused great sadness among the religious of her community...."She was part of our lives and, as you can well understand, in a Carmelite convent, in a cloistered life, one is in contact 24 hours a day." Speaking about the future without the visionary's presence, Sister Maria Celina expressed the certainty that "she is with us in another way.... Passing by her cell, one feels like going in, but she is

no longer there, not there at the sensible level understood by our nature, but we know in faith that she is with us."[75]

Nevertheless, Sister Lucia's death may still have far-reaching effects. The prioress thought an eventual flowering of vocations to the contemplative life, motivated by the example of the little shepherdess's life, could be possible. "It might happen. God makes use of everything. It is he who calls.... It was no accident that my vocation was born when I heard talk about the house where the little shepherdess lived only to pray, and I said, 'I also want to be like that.'"

Sister Lucia died surrounded by her sisters in religion, along with the bishop of Coimbra, her doctors, and the nurse. Her last words were:

"For the Holy Father!... Our Lady, Our Lady, Holy Angels, Heart of Jesus, Heart of Jesus! We are going, we are going."

"Where?" asked Sister Maria Celina.

"To Heaven."

"With whom?" asked Sister Celina

"With Our Lord ... Our Lady ... and the little Shepherds. Let us go! Let me go!"

And she breathed her last.

Sister Lucia's death had a great impact on Portugal. February 15, 2005, was declared a day of national mourning; even campaigning for the national parliamentary election, scheduled for February 20, was interrupted. A guard of honor surrounded her coffin: thirty-five bishops from Portugal, the seventeen nuns of Sister Lucia's community, her family members, and many of the Portuguese people attended to say farewell to this great messenger in the Church.

There is so much more that could be written about the long life and mission of Sister Lucia. Through her great love for Our Lord and Our Lady, she was able to share with the world a message that remains more relevant and necessary today than ever before.

CHAPTER 7

THE CONSECRATION OF RUSSIA

The first mention of the consecration of Russia was part of the secret the Mother of Jesus revealed to the three shepherd children on July 13, 1917. At that time, she foretold terrible suffering for the whole world, including war, hunger, and persecution of the Church and the Holy Father. To prevent these punishments, Our Lady asked for the consecration of Russia and the Communion of reparation on First Saturdays. Otherwise, she warned, the errors of Russia would spread throughout the world. At that time, the Russian Communist Revolution had just begun.

The consecration and its significance for the world, however, can be understood only in light of the final apparition of Our Lady to Lucia on June 13, 1929, during her time in Tuy, Spain. This "last" apparition is important for two reasons. First, the vision in itself provided a summary of the essentials of our Catholic faith. Second, Our Lady's concluding words concern the future of the world. Namely, Mary's instruction to Sister Lucia was clear: "The moment has come when God asks the Holy Father, in union with all the bishops of the world, to make the Consecration of Russia to my Heart, promising to save it by this means."[76]

During the decades after 1917, with the Bolshevik revolution, the evils of an atheistic system spread worldwide. We now understand this was because the world had not been consecrated as Mary had asked. She had promised: "In the end, my Immaculate Heart will triumph. The Holy Father will consecrate Russia to me and it will be converted, and a time of peace will be conceded to the world."[77] Sadly, it would be many decades before the consecration was made correctly in 1984.

Controversy

Throughout the years, controversy surrounding the consecration of Russia to the Immaculate Heart has caused considerable confusion among many Catholics who have embraced the message of Fatima. Some have claimed that Pope John Paul II's consecration on March 25, 1984, was invalid because he did not specify Russia in the words of consecration. There has been a good deal of written material critical of the Holy See and the involved cardinals and bishops, including Bishop Alberto Amaral, who had direct contact with Sister Lucia. Yet, on numerous occasions, Sister Lucia declared that Our Lady had accepted the 1984 consecration.

Nonetheless, some continue to argue that the consecration must not have fulfilled Our Lady's wishes, because the time of peace has not yet come. This point of view originates from a misunderstanding of the true nature of the peace Our Lady promised. Her message points to devotion to her Immaculate Heart. She promised, "If what I say to you is done, many souls will be saved and there will be peace."[78] Peace has been promised as a result of living the message of Fatima, which means living our faith. When we do, peace in our conscience, peace with God, peace in our homes, peace within families, peace with our neighbors, and ultimately peace between nations will be the result.

Consecrations through the Years

The Consecration on March 25, 1984, was not the Church's first attempt to fulfill the request made by Our Lady of the Rosary at Fatima. On October 31, 1942, Pope Pius XII consecrated the world to the Immaculate Heart of Mary. On July 7, 1952, Pope Pius XII consecrated the Russian people to the Immaculate Heart. In both cases, however, the pope made the consecration alone, without the bishops. On November 21, 1964, Pope Paul VI renewed Pius XII's consecration of Russia to the Immaculate Heart. This was at the Second Vatican Council, promulgating the Dogmatic Constitution on the Church with its eighth chapter on Mary. But once again, though he was in the presence of the Council bishops, the Holy Father acted alone. In each case, Sister Lucia insisted that heaven required it to be a collegial act of the whole Church — pope and bishops together.

On the Feast of Fatima, May 13, 1982, Pope John Paul II went to Fatima to thank Our Lady for saving him from the attempted assassination exactly one year earlier. There he attempted the collegial consecration again. Still again, Sister Lucia said it did not fulfill all the conditions required by God. (Some reports were that not all bishops received the invitation in time to join the pope in the act of consecration or simply did not participate.)

On March 25, 1984, Pope John Paul II was finally joined by a moral totality of Catholic bishops throughout the world in consecrating the world, and therefore Russia, to the Immaculate Heart of Mary. This time, to make certain all bishops were properly informed in advance, the pope sent a request in December 1983 to the bishops of the world to join him in the act in March 1984. The very words of the consecration stated it was intended to renew the previous acts of consecration by Pius XII of the world (1942) and of Russia (1952).

After the March 25, 1984, consecration, the papal nuncio of Lisbon went to Coimbra to see Sister Lucia at her monastery. She told him: "Our Lady has accepted it."

He replied, "Good. Now we await the miracle."[79]

The Fall of Soviet Communism

Lucia kept quiet on the subject, knowing that she had accomplished the mission given to her by God. Meanwhile, almost immediately after March 25, 1984, things began to change in Russia. On the Feast of Our Lady of Fatima, May 13, 1984, an explosion in Severomorsk, Russia, destroyed 80 percent of Russia's missiles, rendering them no longer a superpower. The extent of this explosion was not known in the United States at the time. There was another strange happening on December 13, 1984: an explosion in Siberia destroyed Russia's largest ammunition base. On December 19, Marshal Ustinov, the Soviet minister of defense, died, and three days later Marshal Sodolov, the second minister of defense died.

In March 1985 (one year after the consecration), President Chernenko died and Mikhial Gorbachev was made president of the Soviet Union. He was the first baptized Christian to become president of the USSR, although he remained a Communist. He instituted *glasnost* (openness to the world) and *perestroika* (restructuring of the Soviet economy) and allowed increased freedom of the press and freedom of religion. These innovations were truly the downfall of atheistic communism, and, as a result, fifteen republics were liberated.

In 1989, Sister Lucia knew she must get the message out to the world that the collegial consecration of Russia for its conversion was accomplished. While things had been softening from hard Communism in Russia since 1984, greater things were now about to happen. In the summer of 1989, Sister Lucia said publicly that the consecration was completed and that "God will keep His Word." On November 9 of that year, the Berlin Wall came down without a single shot fired, and Gorbachev met with Pope John Paul II at the Vatican and promised religious freedom.

"It Is Accomplished"

When asked why she waited five years to tell the world that the consecration needed for the conversion of Russia had indeed been accomplished in 1984, Lucia answered, "I don't write for the newspapers, I don't talk on the radio." She had done her duty by informing the nuncio.

Still, some claim the collegial consecration of Russia never occurred. They point to the evils and wars in the world today as proof that Russia's consecration did not happen. Sadly, there are those who choose to ignore or deny what the Vatican has stated and the words of Sister Lucia herself on the matter: "It is accomplished."

We should also keep in mind the relationship between Sister Lucia and Pope Saint John Paul II. Surely, the Holy Father would have confided to her the format of the consecration he planned to use, especially knowing that Our Lady did not accept his attempted consecration in 1982. Below are the actual words of the consecration. Notes are provided throughout for greater clarity.

Act of Collegial Consecration
of the World and Russia in Particular
by Pope John Paul II and the World's Bishops
on March 25, 1984

1. *"We have recourse to your protection, holy Mother of God." As we utter the words of this antiphon with which the Church of Christ has prayed for centuries, we find ourselves today before you, Mother, in the Jubilee Year of the Redemption.*

We find ourselves united with all the Pastors of the Church in a particular bond whereby we constitute a body and a college [the pope here is careful to emphasize the collegiality of the act], *just as by Christ's wish the Apostles constituted a body and college with Peter. In the bond of this union, we utter the words of the present Act, in which we wish to include, once more, the Church's hopes and anxieties for the modern world.*

Forty years ago and again ten years later [in 1952 Pope Pius XII mentioned Russia by name, and this consecration acknowledges it], *your servant Pope Pius XII, having before his eyes the painful experiences of the human family, entrusted and consecrated to your Immaculate Heart the whole world, especially the peoples for which by reason of their situation you have particular love and solicitude.*

This world of individuals and nations we too have before our eyes today: the world of the second millennium that is drawing to a close, the modern world, our world!

The Church, mindful of the Lord's words: "Go ... and make disciples of all nations ... and lo, I am with you always, to the close of the age" (Mt 28:19–20), has, at the Second Vatican Council, given fresh life to her awareness of her mission in this world.

And therefore, O Mother of individuals and peoples, you who know all their sufferings and their hopes, you who have a mother's awareness of all the struggles between good and evil, between light and darkness, which afflict the modern world, accept the cry which we, moved by the Holy Spirit, address directly to your Heart. Embrace, with the love of the Mother and Handmaid of the Lord, this human world of ours, which we entrust and consecrate to you, for we are full of concern for the earthly and eternal destiny of individuals and peoples.

In a special way we entrust and consecrate to you those individuals and nations which particularly need to be thus entrusted and consecrated. [For those acquainted with the message of Fatima, clearly Russia and those countries where Russia had especially spread her errors must have been at the top of the Holy Father's mind. Think about this point: What about the countries that had fallen into Russia's errors — wouldn't they need to be consecrated also, especially since the consecration came so late, allowing Russia's errors to spread. By 1981, 73 percent of the world was living under Communism.]

"We have recourse to your protection, holy Mother of God": despise not our petitions in our necessities.

2. Behold, as we stand before you, Mother of Christ, before your Immaculate Heart, we desire, together with the whole Church, to unite ourselves with the consecration which, for love of us, Your Son made of Himself to the Father: "For their sake," He said, "I consecrate myself that they also may be consecrated in the truth" (Jn 17:19). We wish to unite ourselves with our Redeemer in this His consecration for the world and for the human race, which, in His divine Heart, has the power to obtain pardon and to secure reparation.

The power of this consecration lasts for all time and embraces all individuals, peoples and nations. It overcomes every evil that the spirit of darkness is able to awaken, and has in fact awakened in our times, in the heart of man and in his history.

How deeply we feel the need for the consecration of humanity and the world — our modern world — in union with Christ Himself! For the redeeming work of Christ must be shared in by the world through the Church.

The present Year of the Redemption shows this: the special Jubilee of the whole Church. Above all creatures, may you be blessed, you, the Handmaid of the Lord, who in the fullest way obeyed the divine call!

Hail to you, who are wholly united to the redeeming consecration of your Son!

Mother of the Church! Enlighten the People of God along the paths of faith, hope and love! Help us to live in the truth of the consecration of Christ for the entire human family of the modern world.

3. In entrusting to you, O Mother, the world, all individuals and peoples, we also entrust to you this very consecration of the world, placing it in your motherly Heart.

Immaculate Heart! Help us to conquer the menace of evil, which so easily takes root in the hearts of the people of today, and whose immeasurable effects already weigh down upon our modern world and seem to block the paths towards the future!

From famine and war, deliver us.

From nuclear war, from incalculable self-destruction, from every kind of war, deliver us.

From sins against the life of man from its very beginning, deliver us.

From hatred and from the demeaning of the dignity of the children of God, deliver us.

From every kind of injustice in the life of society, both national and international, deliver us.

From readiness to trample on the commandments of God, deliver us.

From attempts to stifle in human hearts the very truth of God, deliver us.

From the loss of awareness of good and evil, deliver us.

From sins against the Holy Spirit, deliver us, deliver us.

Accept, O Mother of Christ, this cry laden with the sufferings of all individual human beings, laden with the sufferings of whole societies. Help us with the power of the Holy Spirit to conquer all sin: individual sin and the "sin of the world," sin in all its manifestations.

> *Let there be revealed, once more in the history of the world, the infinite saving power of the Redemption: the power of merciful Love! May it put a stop to evil! May it transform consciences! May your Immaculate Heart reveal for all the light of Hope!*

Further Proof

Those who say that the consecration was not done have sometimes tried to tarnish the reputations of good priests and laity, even those who have made the message of Fatima their life's mission. A year after she went public in 1989, Sister Lucia wrote a personal letter to the late Father Robert J. Fox. That letter has been widely circulated and published several times. It is on display at the Father Robert J. Fox and Our Lady of Fatima Museum in Hanceville, Alabama. The signature, written in pen by Sister Lucia, was analyzed by a graphologist who confirmed that the signature was authentic. Below is a copy of the letter in Portuguese and then translated into English.

J. † M.
Pax Christi
Rev. do Sr. P. Robert J. Fox

> *Recebi a sua carta e venho responder á sua pregunta: «Se a Consagração feita por Jão Paulo II, em 25 de Março de 1984, em união com todos os Bispos do mondo, cumpriu as codições para a coversão da Russia, segundo o pedido de Nossa Senhora em Tuy a 13 de Junho de 1929.»? Sim, compriu, e desde aí, eu tenho dito que está feita.*

E digo que não é nenhuma outra pessoa que responde por mim, sou eu quem recebe a correspondência, abre as cartas e responde.

Em união de orações.
Coimbra, 3-VII-1990
Irmã Lúcia

(Translation)

J. † M.
The Peace of Christ
Rev. Father Robert J. Fox

I come to answer your question, "If the consecration made by Pope John Paul II on March 25, 1984, in union with all the bishops of the world, accomplished the condition for the conversion of Russia, according to the request of Our Lady in Tuy on June 13, 1929."? Yes, it was accomplished, and since then I have said that it was made.

And I say that no other person responds for me, it is I who receive and open all letters and respond to them.

In union of prayers.
Coimbra, July 3, 1990
Sister Lucia

Further Effects of the Consecration

On the Feast of Fatima, May 13, 1990, freedom of religion was made the law of Russia. On the anniversary of the miracle of the sun at Fatima, October 13, in the same year, Mikhail Gorbachev received the Nobel Peace Prize.

Two months later, Gorbachev met the pope at the Vatican for a second time. It has been rumored that in this meeting Pope John Paul II revealed that he knew it was Gorbachev who had ordered the assassination attempt in 1981, and that Gorbachev asked his forgiveness. (Also that it was this story Lucia was asked to keep silent about and nothing else.)

Events continued to unfold in 1991. On May 13, Pope John Paul II went to Fatima to thank Our Lady for all the countries that were liberated, for saving his life, and for the end of the Communist threat to Europe and West Asia. On August 19, the Communists attempted to overthrow Gorbachev. They picked the wrong day, for it was the seventy-fourth anniversary of the August apparition of Our Lady at Fatima. On August 22 (the Feast of the Queenship of Mary), the coup was crushed and the Communists were defeated. Two months later, on October 13, the first pilgrims from Russia went to Fatima. Their journey was broadcast on 150 television stations and 350 radio stations in Russia. Diplomatic relations between the Vatican and Russia were opened in 1991, and Latin-rite churches were allowed to exist in Russia for the first time in decades. On December 8, the Solemnity of Mary's Immaculate Conception, the USSR dissolved peacefully and the regime of the Commonwealth of Independent States began. Twelve days later, Boris Yeltsin met with Pope John Paul II in Rome. On December 25, the Communist hammer and sickle flag came down for last time over Russia. Gorbachev resigned and sent a letter to Pope John Paul II.

At the very end of the year, on December 30, 1991, Lucia wrote that the world would recognize that the defeat of Communism was accomplished by Our Lady.

Most significant of all, on Christmas day in 1992, Communism was declared illegal in Russia.

More Grace to Come

Many changes have occurred since John Paul II's consecration of the world — and Russia — to the Immaculate Heart. The consecration concerned the unity of the faithful in the mystical Body of Christ, and, over time, those who were most closely involved in the act of consecration could see the changes that were taking place. Much more can happen, but we must do our part in living the message of Fatima.

It is not difficult to do so. Praying the Rosary for peace sounds too easy. So, we often neglect Mary's request and disregard the promises she made concerning her special prayer. Some of us think that Eucharistic adoration and reparation take too much time, or that we are too busy to observe the First Saturdays. We are free to respond, or not. The Church does not bind us to observe specific devotions, or even to accept the miraculous apparitions that are approved. But if we want to grow closer to God and help bring peace to the world, our Blessed Mother provides a clear pathway. At Fatima, she made clear what forms of reparation and devotion she loves most.

At the request of her confessor, Sister Lucia asked Jesus why He required the collegial consecration. The answer she received in prayer was so that the world would recognize the powerful intercession of His Mother's Immaculate Heart.

CHAPTER 8

THE SECRET OF FATIMA

The First Two Parts

In 1941, while she was in Tuy, Spain, Sister Lucia was given permission from heaven to reveal the first two parts of the Fatima secret. As she wrote in her third memoir: "The Secret is composed of three different parts, two of which I will go on to reveal. The first is the vision of hell!"

The children were shaken by the vision of hell. Lucia wrote after the vision: "How can we ever be grateful enough to our kind heavenly Mother, who had already prepared us by promising, in the first apparition, to take us to heaven? Otherwise, I think we would have died of fear and terror." Lucia wrote that Jacinta was especially affected by the vision of hell and souls going there: "The vision of hell filled her with horror to such a degree, that every penance and mortification was as nothing in her eyes, if it could only prevent souls from going there."

The vision of hell literally changed the lives of the three children. This vision and first secret gave them strength to be more cautious, to do penance, and to offer up their sacrifices for the conversion of sinners. Around this time Our Lady also taught the children the powerful prayer that we use today at the end of each decade of the rosary: "O my Jesus, forgive us our sins, save us from the fires of hell and lead all souls to heaven, especially those who are in most need of thy mercy."

The second part of the secret refers to the devotion to the Immaculate Heart of Mary. As Lucia explains:

> As I have already written in the second account, Our Lady, on June 13, 1917, told me she would never forsake me and her Immaculate Heart would be my refuge and the road which would lead me to God. With these last words, she opened her hands and pierced our hearts with the light that streamed from her palms. It seems that, on that day, the first purpose of this light was to give us a special knowledge and love for the Immaculate Heart of Mary just as on the two other occasions it gave us a better knowledge of God and the mystery of the Holy Trinity. From that day on we felt in our hearts a deeper love for the Immaculate Heart of Mary.[80]

This message was not just for the three shepherd children, but for all of us. The Mother of Christ still invites each one of us to join personally with the Church in consecration to her Immaculate Heart.

The Third Part

The third part of the secret of Fatima was not revealed publicly until May 13, 2000, when Pope John Paul II traveled to Fatima for the beatifications of Jacinta and Francisco. During that Jubilee Year, Fatima was the only place outside of Italy, besides the Holy Land, to which the pope traveled. Unfortunately, there continues to be a lot of confusion surrounding the "third secret" and its revelation. While Sister Lucia herself said that the secret had been revealed in its entirety, some still speculate that the Church has held part of the secret back. As we shall see, there is no evidence to support this idea.

Sister Lucia wrote out the third part of the secret in 1944, at the order of her bishop, when she was very ill. The document was then kept in the Vatican's secret archives by the Congregation for the Doctrine of the Faith for many years. Lucia found it difficult to put the third part of the secret in writing and was torn within herself. She did not want to disobey the bishop, but she feared she was disobeying the Blessed Mother, as she had been told not to reveal it to anyone. Even though the Church planned to keep the document safe, it seemed to her it would not have the protection of secrecy once it was in writing, since it could be released or discovered by others. Finally, Our Blessed Mother appeared to Sister Lucia and told her to do as the bishop requested. The document would be adequately protected in the secret archives of the Vatican. Once the Blessed Mother told her to do as the bishop requested, Lucia wrote as follows:

**The Third Part of the Secret
Written by Sister Lucia
by Order of the Bishop of Leiria
and the Most Holy Mother
on January 3, 1944**

J.M.J.

The third part of the secret revealed at the Cova da Iria-Fatima, on 13 July 1917.

I write in obedience to you, my God, who command me to do so through his Excellency the Bishop of Leiria and through your Most Holy Mother and mine.

After the two parts which I have already explained, at the left of Our Lady and a little above, we saw an Angel with a flaming sword in his left hand; flashing, it gave out flames that looked as though they would set the world on fire; but they died out in contact with the splendor that Our Lady radiated towards him from her right hand; pointing to the earth with his right hand, the Angel cried out in a loud voice: "Penance, Penance, Penance!" And we saw in an immense light that is God: something similar to how people appear in a mirror when they pass in front of it "a Bishop dressed in White" — we had the impression that it was the Holy Father. Other Bishops, Priests, men and women Religious going up a steep mountain, at the top of which there was a big Cross of rough-hewn trunks as of a cork-tree with the bark; before reaching there the Holy Father passed through a big city half in ruins and half trembling with halting step, afflicted with pain and sorrow, he prayed for the souls of the corpses he met on his way; having reached the top of the mountain, on his knees at the foot of the big Cross he was killed by a group of soldiers who fired bullets and arrows at him, and in the same way there died one after another the other Bishops, Priests, men and women Religious, and various lay people of different ranks and positions. Beneath the two arms of the Cross there were two Angels each with a crystal aspersorium in his hand, in which they gathered up the blood of the Martyrs and with it sprinkled the souls that were making their way to God.[81]

The official translation of the first and second parts of the secret presented by Sister Lucia in the third memoir of August 31, 1941, for the bishop of Leiria-Fatima, and that of the third part of the secret written on January 3,

1944, appeared in the Vatican document, "The Message of Fatima — The Third Secret." Along with an English translation of the three parts of the secret, the Vatican Congregation for the Doctrine of the Faith presented all three parts in photocopies of Sister Lucia's actual handwriting in the Portuguese language. The final words of the Vatican commentary say: "In the translation, the original text has been respected, even as regards the imprecise punctuation, which nevertheless does not impede an understanding of what the visionary wished to say."

Cardinal Angelo Sodano, then Vatican secretary of state, announced at Fatima on May 13, 2000, in the presence of His Holiness Pope John Paul II and Sister Lucia, that the pope had charged the Congregation for the Doctrine of the Faith with making public the third part of the Fatima secret after an appropriate commentary had been prepared.

Cardinal Joseph Ratzinger (now Pope Emeritus Benedict XVI), served as the prefect of that congregation at the time. On June 26, 2000, all three parts of the Fatima secret were released to the public along with commentary in a document entitled "The Message of Fatima." While the commentary of the Congregation of the Doctrine of the Faith is quoted below, the following words of Cardinal Sodano at Fatima will help introduce it:

> The vision of Fatima concerns above all the war waged by atheist systems against the Church and Christians, and it describes the immense suffering endured by the witnesses to the faith in the last century of the second millennium. It is an interminable Way of the Cross, led by the Popes of the twentieth century.

According to the interpretation of the little shepherds, which was also recently confirmed by Sister Lucia, the bishop clothed in white who prays for all the faithful is the Pope. As he makes his way with great effort toward the Cross, amid the corpses of those who are martyred — bishops, priests, men and women religious and many lay persons — he too falls to the ground, apparently dead, under the burst of gunfire.

After the assassination attempt of May 13, 1981, it appeared evident to His Holiness that it was "a motherly hand which guided the bullet's path, enabling the dying Pope to halt at the threshold of death" (Pope John Paul II, Meditation from the Policlinico Gemelli to the Italian Bishops, Insegnamenti, XVII, 1 [1994], 1061).[82]

According to the commentary by the Congregation for the Doctrine of the Faith: "The martyrs die in communion with the Passion of Christ, and their death becomes one with his. For the sake of the body of Christ, they complete what is still lacking in his afflictions (cf. Col 1:24). Their life has itself become a Eucharist, part of the mystery of the grain of wheat which in dying yields abundant fruit. The blood of the martyrs is the seed of Christians, said Tertullian. As from Christ's death, from His wounded side, the Church was born, so the death of the witnesses is fruitful for the future life of the Church."

As Pope John Paul II himself said: "The new generations must know the cost of the faith they have inherited, if they are to receive the torch of the Gospel with gratitude and shed its light on the new century and the new millennium."[83]

The twentieth century saw clearly the cost of the faith of which Pope John Paul II spoke. Before and during the Second World War, Nazis killed six million Jews in concentration camps. Millions of others, including Christians, were also killed. Some three thousand Catholic priests were interned in Dachau. After the Second World War, Communist persecutions became systematic in Eastern Europe. Seeing all of this, Pope John Paul II concluded that "countless numbers refused to yield to the cult of the false gods of the twentieth century and were sacrificed by Communism, Nazism, by the idolatry of State or race."[84] Fatima provided a warning ahead of time, and it is a warning we, too, would do well to consider in our own day.

Was the Entirety of the Third Part of the Fatima Secret Released?

The Vatican released the third and final part of the Fatima secret with commentary, on the order of Pope John Paul II, on June 26, 2000. Nevertheless, some controversy has developed around this third part of the secret. There are those who believe that only some of the third secret was released in June 2000, and that a portion of it is still being held back. Decades before the third part was released, wild reports of what it contained circulated publicly. None of these were the least bit credible to anyone who knew Fatima in depth.

Unfortunately, speculations remain that the third part of the secret, as released by the Congregation for the Doctrine of the Faith, was either incomplete or incorrect. Some claim the third part of the Fatima secret was contained in two separate documents — a diary description and a separate sheet containing Mary's actual words.

They argue that only the diary document was released on June 26, 2000, and the sheet containing the words of Our Lady remains secret. Generally, proponents of these theories are people who are disappointed that the Vatican text does not speak about the end of the world or warn the Church about this catastrophe.

What we do know is that Pope Pius XII kept a brief, single-sheet message containing Mary's words, dated by Sister Lucia on or immediately prior to January 9, 1944, in a wooden safe in his apartment. This fact was attested to by Sister Pasqualina, who served Pope Pius XII. Pope John Paul II read the document after his election to the papacy. The four-page diary description, dated January 3, 1944, was kept in the archives of the Congregation for the Doctrine of the Faith (then called the Holy Office). It was read on August 17, 1959, by Pope John XXIII and by John Paul II after the attempt on his life in 1981.

Sister Lucia herself discredited all claims that any part of Fatima's secret remained withheld. On April 27, 2000, Sister Lucia met in the Coimbra monastery with Archbishop Tarcisio Bertone, secretary of the Congregation for the Doctrine of the Faith, and Bishop Serafim de Sousa Ferreira e Silva, the bishop of Leiria-Fatima. Pope John Paul II could not attend in person, but sent the following letter as an introduction to the April 27 meeting:

> *To the Reverend Sr. MARIA LUCIA of the Convent of Coimbra.*
>
> *In the great joy of Easter, I greet you with the word the Risen Jesus spoke to the disciples: "Peace be with you!"*
> *I will be happy to be able to meet you on the long-awaited day of the Beatification of Francisco*

and Jacinta, which, please God, I will celebrate on 13 May of this year.

Since on that day there will be time only for a brief greeting and not a conversation, I am sending His Excellency Archbishop Tarcisio Bertone, Secretary of the Congregation for the Doctrine of the Faith, to speak with you. This is the Congregation which works most closely with the Pope in defending the true Catholic faith, and which since 1957, as you know, has kept your hand-written letter containing the third part of the "secret" revealed on 13 July 1917 at Cova da Iria, Fatima.

Archbishop Bertone, accompanied by the Bishop of Leiria, His Excellency Bishop Serafim de Sousa Ferreira e Silva, will come in my name to ask certain questions about the interpretation of "the third part of the secret."

Sister Maria Lucia, you may speak openly and candidly to Archbishop Bertone, who will report your answers directly to me.

I pray fervently to the Mother of the Risen Lord for you, Reverend Sr., for the Community of Coimbra and for the whole Church. May Mary, Mother of pilgrim humanity, keep us always united to Jesus, her beloved Son and our brother, the Lord of life and glory.

With my special Apostolic Blessing.
JOANNES PAULUS PP. II
From the Vatican, 19 April 2000

The meeting was a fruitful one. As the official commentary on the Message of Fatima and the third part of the secret states:

The Bishop of Leiria-Fatima read the autograph letter of the Holy Father to Sister Lucia which explained the reasons for the visit. Sister Lucia felt honored by this and reread the letter herself, contemplating it in her own hands. She said that she was prepared to answer all questions frankly.

At this point, Archbishop Bertone presented two envelopes to her; the first containing the second, which held the third part of the "secret" of Fatima. Immediately, touching it with her fingers, she said: "This is my letter," and then while reading it: "This is my writing."[85]

The official commentary on Fatima and its secret issued by the Congregation for the Doctrine of the Faith under the direction of Cardinal Ratzinger continues as follows:

> The original text, in Portuguese, was read and interpreted with the help of the Bishop of Leiria-Fatima. Sister Lucia agreed with the interpretation that the third part of the "secret" was a prophetic vision, similar to those in sacred history. She repeated her conviction that the vision of Fatima concerns above all the struggle of atheistic Communism against the Church and against Christians, and describes the terrible sufferings of the victims of the faith in the twentieth century.
>
> When asked: "Is the principal figure in the vision the Pope?" Sister Lucia replied at once that it was. She recalled that the three children were very sad about the suffering of the Pope, and that Jacinta kept saying: *"Coitandinho do Santo Padre, tenho muita pena dos pecadores!"* ("Poor Holy Father, I

am very sad for sinners!"). Sister Lucia continued: "We did not know the name of the Pope; Our Lady did not tell us the name of the Pope; we did not know whether it was Benedict XV or Pius XII or Paul VI or John Paul II; but it was the Pope who was suffering and that made us suffer too."

As regards the passage about the Bishop dressed in white, this is, the Holy Father — as the children immediately realized during the "vision" — who is struck dead and falls to the ground, Sister Lucia was in full agreement with the Pope's claim that "it was a mother's hand that guided the bullet's path and in his throes the Pope halted at the threshold of death" (Pope John Paul II, Meditation from the Policlinico Gemelli to the Italian Bishops, 13 May 1994).

Before giving the sealed envelope containing the third part of the "secret" to the then Bishop of Leiria-Fatima, Sister Lucia wrote on the outside envelope that it could be opened only after 1960, either by the Patriarch of Lisbon or the Bishop of Leiria. Archbishop Bertone therefore asked, "Why only after 1960? Was it Our Lady who fixed that date?" Sister Lucia replied: "It was not Our Lady. I fixed the date because I had the intuition that before 1960 it would not be understood, but that only later would it be understood. Now it can be better understood. I wrote down what I saw; however it was not for me to interpret it, but for the pope."[86]

Sister Lucia recognized her role clearly: she was only the messenger of Fatima, not the interpreter. She yielded to the pope as the true interpreter of the visions she and her cousins saw. The detailed commentary on the Fatima secret, issued by the Congregation for the Doctrine of the Faith upon the order of Pope John Paul II, should be accepted as complete — just as the release itself says it is.

In the commentary, then Cardinal Joseph Ratzinger touched on the controversy surrounding the third part:

> A careful reading of the text of the so-called third "secret" of Fatima, published here in its entirety long after the fact and by decision of the Holy Father, will probably prove disappointing or surprising after all the speculation it has stirred. No great mystery is revealed; nor is the future unveiled. We see the Church of the martyrs of the century which has just passed represented in a scene described in a language which is symbolic and not easy to decipher. Is this what the Mother of the Lord wished to communicate to Christianity and to humanity at a time of great difficulty and distress? Is it of any help to us at the beginning of the new millennium? Or are these only projections of the inner world of children, brought up in a climate of profound piety but shaken at the same time by the tempests which threatened their own time? How should we understand the vision? What are we to make of it?[87]

Then Cardinal Ratzinger satisfactorily handled these questions in the commentary. His prediction when he prepared the commentary proved accurate. Yet the disappointment and suspicions surrounding the release of the "third secret" arise from a failure to look at the Fatima message as a whole. The third part of the secret must be understood relative to the first two parts, and to the whole Fatima message.

People who are new to the message of Fatima may find these controversies disheartening. That is why it is important to address them. Those who claim the entire secret was not released in 2000 are merely spinning conjectures and conspiracy theories. Worse, they are promoting a viewpoint that is not in harmony with the pope, the Congregation for the Doctrine of the Faith, or Sister Lucia herself. There are no substantial verifications of these claims.

The Fatima revelations accurately described the twentieth century as a century of martyrs, suffering, persecution of the Church, world wars, and numerous local conflicts. Nevertheless, Cardinal Ratzinger's commentary did seem to indicate that the third part of the secret did not deal merely with the past. In fact, he made it clear that private revelation often contains a message not just for the present, but also for the future. In his comments on Fatima, he shows the way the Church must tread in our time of violence, destruction, and persecution.

Sister Lucia shared her thoughts:

> The third part of the secret refers to Our Lady's words: "If not [Russia] will spread her errors throughout the world, causing wars and persecutions of the Church. The good will be martyred; the Holy Father will have much to suffer; various nations will be annihilated" (13-VII-1917).
>
> The third part of the secret is a symbolic revelation, referring to this part of the Message, conditioned by whether we accept or not what

the Message itself asks of us: "If my requests are heeded, Russia will be converted, and there will be peace; if not, she will spread her errors throughout the world, etc."

Since we did not heed this appeal of the Message, we see that it has been fulfilled, Russia has invaded the world with her errors. And if we have not yet seen the complete fulfillment of the final part of this prophecy, we are going towards it little by little with great strides. If we do not reject the path of sin, hatred, revenge, injustice, violations of the rights of the human person, immorality and violence, etc.[88]

Why did such a short and simple text as the third part of the Fatima secret need to be so carefully guarded for all those decades? For an answer, we need only to look back at the violent history of the twentieth century. It takes little imagination to see how unstable individuals might have attempted to "fulfill" the secret, perhaps more than once, had it been released any sooner. In fact, Mehmet Agca, the Turkish terrorist who attempted to assassinate John Paul II, stated immediately after the release of the secret that he merely attempted to carry out what was destined by providence.

The key element we must remember in reading this third part of Fatima's secret is that it is still for all of us, even now. Its purpose is to remind us that as Christians we are promised persecution, and that this persecution is not limited to one time or place. The Fatima message is meant to give us the strength and the grace we need to face this reality in our daily lives. Mary wants to help us. That's why she asked for widespread devotion to her Immaculate Heart. Christian persecution and suffering will persist, but through Our Lady's intercession, we can be assured of true and lasting peace as well as ultimate triumph.

CHAPTER 9

LIVING THE MESSAGE OF FATIMA

Our Lady's appearances in Portugal were not just for the people of Portugal or of 1917, or for the three little shepherds. Mary has a message for all of us, one that invites each of us to enter more deeply into our call as baptized Catholics. Fatima offers us key insights into the essential elements of our faith. Our Lady has given us the tools to help us in our spiritual journey and to counteract the evil we face in the world and in our own lives. While Catholics are not required to believe in Fatima's apparitions or message, all are invited to do so. Those who have put the message of Fatima into practice have discovered a grace-filled framework for spiritual growth.

We have seen the power of Mary's instruction at Fatima most clearly in the lives of the three children who saw her. Although they were so young, Francisco and Jacinta Marto demonstrated heroic Christian virtue during their short lives. They were beatified by Pope John Paul II in the jubilee year of 2000 and canonized by Pope Francis on May 13, 2017, during the celebration of the centennial of the Fatima apparitions. Francisco and Jacinta are the youngest nonmartyrs in the history of the Church to be declared saints. Sister Lucia's process to beatification is also gaining traction. Recently, fifteen thousand letters, testimonies, and other supporting documents have been sent to the Vatican's Congregation for the Causes of the Saints for approval. In order to proceed to the next step, the documents must also be reviewed by Pope Francis.

In many ways, the Fatima apparitions early in the twentieth century were preparing the Church for the evils of our times. Abortion, the rise of sexual deviance and promiscuity, adultery, murder, violence, drug use, and many other grave evils are commonplace in our society: these deadly sins offend Our Lord very much. The three children noted that Our Lady always looked very sad when she appeared to them: she only smiled once. Mary's Immaculate Heart has been pierced by our sins. She appeared at Fatima to lead us back to God and to the peace that only comes through reconciliation with God.

Really, Mary's requests at Fatima were nothing new; she was simply asking us to rekindle our devotion to her Son. Ultimately, if we do what she asks, we open ourselves to receive the graces we need to live as Christians. Five of the requests Our Lady made through the three children are devotions and practices all of us can make a part of our lives. They are: praying the Rosary, ideally every day; offering our actions and sufferings to Jesus; observing the five First Saturdays; devotion to the Immaculate Heart; and wearing the brown scapular.

Pray the Rosary Daily

At the beginning of the apparitions, the Blessed Mother told the children to pray the Rosary every day for peace. She stressed the importance and power of the holy Rosary. When Our Lady told the children to pray the Rosary every day, she was urging all of us to do the same. I know that praying the Rosary has changed my life, and I have seen it work miracles in the lives of others.

We have seen amazing signs of the fulfillment of our Blessed Mother's promises about the power of prayer, especially the Rosary. Many battles have been won throughout history through the power of this prayer, and it is even more important today. Below are just a few of the miracles that Our Lady has accomplished through the Rosary:

- October 7, 1571 — At the Battle of Lepanto, a greatly outnumbered force of Christian defenders held off a Turkish invasion. It was considered a miraculous victory brought about specifically through the Rosary, for Pope Saint Pius V's crusade united all of Europe in prayer.

- May 13, 1955 — After 700,000 people agreed to pray the Rosary in Austria, the Soviets mysteriously departed the country on the anniversary date of Our Lady's first apparition in Fatima.

- October 13, 1960 — After Pope John XXIII called for prayer, a million pilgrims in Fatima held an all-night prayer vigil in which they prayed the Rosary before the Blessed Sacrament. The next day, the anniversary of the final Fatima apparition, an accident destroyed a new Soviet missile, killing many top scientists and setting back the Soviet nuclear arms program by at least twenty years.

- May 13, 1984 — After another major Rosary crusade, a massive explosion eliminated two-thirds of the missiles of the Soviet Union's powerful Northern Fleet.

- October 12, 1988 — Four years later, it happened again! As thousands prayed the Rosary all night long, on the vigil of the anniversary of the final apparition at Fatima, another major explosion shut down the Soviet Union's only missile plant.

Our Blessed Mother has said that the Rosary is the chain with which she promises to bind Satan: "The Rosary is my Power.... It is the weapon which you must make use of in these times of the Great Battle.... Every Rosary which you recite with me has the effect of restricting the action of the Evil One, of drawing souls away from his pernicious influence ... and of expanding goodness in my children."[89]

Our Lady has shown us that the Rosary can stop wars. In fact, Our Blessed Mother has said that "we can do more in one day of intense prayer, than years of discussion."[90] At Fatima, she urged us to "say the Rosary every day to obtain world peace and an end to war." Are we listening?

Offer Our Sufferings to Jesus

Our Lady asked the children at Fatima, "Are you willing to offer yourselves to God and bear the sufferings He will send you, as an act of reparation for the conversion of sinners? You are going to have much to suffer, but the grace of God will be your comfort." Since Christ conquered all by his cross and resurrection, we know that suffering never has the final say. That is how we can accept whatever challenges we face with absolute trust — trust that God knows not only what's best for us, but for all souls.

Fulfilling our daily duties gives us an opportunity to unite our whole lives to God. Every simple act in our daily lives, even our work and basic chores, can be turned into prayer when we offer them to the Lord. Sickness, annoyances, and other difficulties can become sacrifices that we choose to make for our own souls and for the conversion of sinners. Following Saint Jacinta's example, we can simply give our troubles to the Lord and pray, "It is for you, Jesus, and the conversion of poor sinners." This can become our way of life.

First Saturday Devotion and Devotion to the Immaculate Heart of Mary

Mary promised Lucia in 1917 that she would live many years to spread devotion to the Immaculate Heart. Lucia always attached a lot of importance to the First Saturday devotion as a way to make Mary's Immaculate Heart more known and loved. In Lucia's early letters especially, her intense desire for people to learn about and embrace the devotion of the First Saturdays is striking. Observing the First Saturdays remained very important to her for the rest of her long life as a Carmelite.

For centuries, the Church has designated Saturday as a special day to honor the Mother of God. Votive Masses in honor of Our Blessed Mother are frequently offered on Saturdays if no special liturgical feast of the Church falls on that day. In asking for the devotion of five First Saturdays, Mary articulated that tradition, while infusing it with new life — and an abundance of promised graces.

While the Rosary and the special devotions of First Saturdays are not part of the divine liturgy of the Church, they are certainly related to the liturgy in that they lead to it and depend upon it. First Saturdays are also important for the universal Church, so much so that Mary has attached special promises to their observance. Saint John Paul II considered the First Saturdays so important that, on March 3, 1979, he began the practice of reciting the

Rosary on the Vatican radio station on the First Saturday of every month.

On December 10, 1925, while Lucia was still a Dorothean religious sister in Pontevedra, Spain, the Mother of God appeared to her with the child Jesus at her side. In this apparition, Mary revealed the profound intimacy she desires with each one of us. She rested one of her hands on Lucia's shoulder, "in the other hand she held a Heart surrounded with sharp thorns." The Child Jesus spoke: "Have pity on the Heart of your Most Holy Mother. It is covered with the thorns with which ungrateful men pierce it at every moment, and there is no one to remove them with an act of reparation." Then Our Lady said to Lucia: "My daughter, look at my Heart surrounded with the thorns with which ungrateful men pierce it at every moment by their blasphemies and ingratitude. You, at least, try to console me...."

> The Blessed Mother then asked that faithful Catholics observe five First Saturdays, promising that she would intercede for a happy death for all those who do so. She explained how to keep properly the First Saturdays devotion: "I promise to assist at the hour of death with all the graces necessary for salvation all those who, on the first Saturday of five consecutive months, go to Confession and receive Holy Communion, recite five decades of the Rosary and keep me company for a quarter of an hour while meditating on the mysteries of the Rosary, with the intention of making reparation to me."[91]

Here we see clearly that the call of Fatima is a call to enter more deeply into the most basic practices of our faith.

Our Lady is calling Catholics back to frequent confession, at least once per month, and also to Mass. In the First Saturday devotion, she asks that all of these activities be performed specifically in reparation for sins committed against her Immaculate Heart. Sin causes the entire Church to suffer, but our reparation can increase the glory of the entire Church. This means observing First Saturdays strengthens all the members of the universal Church, not simply oneself.

On February 15, 1926, a little more than two months after the December 10, 1925, apparition, the Child Jesus again appeared to Lucia, asking her if she had spread this devotion. Lucia told the Child Jesus of the difficulties pointed out by her confessor. Her mother superior strongly desired to propagate the devotion, but her confessor warned her that she could do nothing by herself. Jesus replied: "It is true that your superior alone can do nothing, but with my grace she can do all."

Sister Lucia explained what she felt:

> While staying in the chapel with our Lord part of the night, between the 29th and 30th of this month of May 1930, and speaking to our good Lord … I felt myself being more possessed by the divine presence, and if I am not mistaken, the following was revealed to me: "My daughter, the motive is simple: there are 5 ways in which people offend, and blaspheme against the Immaculate Heart of Mary:
>
> 1. The blasphemies against the Immaculate Conception.
>
> 2. Against her virginity.

3. Against her divine maternity, refusing at the same time to accept her as the Mother of all mankind.

4. Those who try publicly to implant in the children's hearts indifference, contempt and even hate against this Immaculate Mother.

5. Those who insult her directly in her sacred statues.

"Here, my daughter, is the motive why the Immaculate Heart of Mary made me ask for this little act of reparation and due to it move my mercy to forgive those souls who had the misfortune of offending her. As for you, try incessantly with all your prayers and sacrifices to move me into mercifulness toward those poor souls."[92]

The late Bishop John Venancio summarized the Fatima message this way: "The Fatima message is reparation, reparation, reparation and especially Eucharistic reparation."[93] The Mass itself is the infinite act of reparation to God the Father for the sins of humanity, as it perpetuates the redeeming sacrifice of the cross. What is reparation? It is making up for sin, which is always a failure in love, by offering greater love. We deprive God of glory when we sin. Reparation restores that glory.

In 1916, when the Angel gave Holy Communion to the three little shepherd children, he taught them to make acts of Eucharistic reparation, especially this powerful prayer: *Most Holy Trinity, Father, Son and Holy Spirit, I adore You profoundly. I offer You the most precious Body, Blood, Soul and Divinity of Jesus Christ, present in all the tabernacles of the world, in reparation for the outrages, sacrileges and indifference by which He is offended. By the infinite merits of the Sacred Heart of Jesus, and the Immaculate Heart of Mary, I beg the conversion of poor sinners.* Our Lady asked that this kind of Eucharistic reparation be made especially on First Saturdays. Even after the 1984 consecration of the world to the Immaculate Heart, Sister Lucia said that the First Saturdays remain important for the more perfect conversion of Russia.

The Brown Scapular

Devotional scapulars are made of two small squares of cloth connected by a band. It is worn over shoulders so that one square of cloth hangs across the chest and the other rests on the back. Mary presented the brown scapular to Saint Simon Stock, an English member of the Carmelite Order, in 1251. At that time, she promised him that "anyone dying in this habit shall not suffer eternal fire."

In the last apparition at Fatima, on October 13, Mary appeared briefly as Our Lady of Mount Carmel. Sister Lucia was once asked about this in an interview. She replied that Mary appeared this way "because Our Lady wants all to wear the Scapular.... The reason for this is that the Scapular is our sign of consecration to the Immaculate Heart of Mary." When asked if the brown scapular is as necessary to the fulfillment of Our Lady's requests as the Rosary, Sister Lucia answered, "The Scapular and the Rosary are inseparable."[94]

Fatima Is for You

The message of Fatima is for all people, and it is just as relevant and important for our faith today as it was one hundred years ago. What Mary and the Angel taught the children at Fatima in 1917 touches on our whole spiritual life today — a life of faith, hope, and love. It is the Holy Spirit inspiring our love of God and one another that purifies us and sanctifies us. We live out this love in our prayer, our acts of reparation, and especially our devotion to Christ and His holy mother, beginning and ending with the Eucharist.

Ultimately, Mary appeared to the three little shepherds to bring us all closer to God as we learn to believe, hope, trust, and love Him. It is now up to us to accept Our Lady's call and learn, live, and share its truths. This message is a message of hope for all of us. Our Lady of Fatima, pray for us! Saint Francisco, Saint Jacinta, and Lucia, pray for us!

PHOTOS

Above left: Jacinta in 1917
Above right: Francisco in 1917

Left: The three shepherd children during the September 13, 1917, apparition. Notice the bright light on the right side of the picture.

Above: The three shepherd children with three local women who believed them from the beginning.

Jacinta during the apparitions.

The well behind Lucia's house where the second apparition of the Angel took place.

People from all over Portugal witnessed the October 13, 1917, Miracle of the Sun.

Original chapel built at the site of the apparitions by local community members.

Above: The orphanage run by Mother Godinho, where Jacinta stayed after developing tuberculosis.

Left: Lucia when she became a Dorothean sister in 1928.

Pope Paul VI, the first pope to visit Fatima, May 13, 1967.

Pope John Paul II in Fatima, May 13, 1991.

*Sister Lucia and the Carmelite sisters admiring the crown
from the statue of Our Lady after the bullet from the John
Paul II assassination attempt was embedded in it.*

Left: Sister Lucia with Dr. Branca Paul, her personal doctor for the last fifteen years of her life, until her death in 2005.

Sister Lucia posing for a picture as a member of the Carmelites.

J. + M.

The Peace of Christ

Rev. Father Robert J. Fox

I come to answer your question, "If the consecration made by Pope John Paul II on March 25, 1984 in union with all the bishops of the world, accomplished the conditions for the conversion of Russia, according to the request of Our Lady in Tuy on June 13 of 1929"? Yes, it was accomplished, and since then I have said that it was made.

And I say that no other person responds for me, it is I who receive and open all letters and respond to them.

In union of prayers.

Coimbra, July 3, 1990

Sister Lucia
(signature)

Translation of Sister Lucia's letter to Father Robert J. Fox.

Know Yourself

FRAN MILLER
Certified Graphoanalyst

GREAT BEND, KANSAS 67530

(316) 793-5568

Handwriting Analysis
Document Examiner
Personnel Assessment

November 24, 1990

Father Robert J. Fox
St/ Mary of Mercy Church
Alexandria, S.D.

Dear Father Fox,

As a Certified Graphoanalyst, I have analyzed the signatures of Sister Lucia, on letters from 1927, to 1990, including a letter to Sister Mary of Bethlehem (Belem) and a letter to you.

All these signatures are consistant and analyzed as written by the same person.

Sincerely,

Fran Miller CGA

Fran Miller, cga

Right: To stop speculation by dissenters, Father Fox had the letter analyzed to confirm that it was Sister Lucia who wrote it.

The Basilica of Our Lady of the Rosary was consecrated in 1953. It is located on the hill in Fatima where Lucia, Francisco, and Jacinta played games while herding their sheep and encountered Our Lady for the first time. It was also the site of the canonization of Jacinta and Francisco by Pope Francis on May 13, 2017, during the celebration of the centennial of the Fatima apparitions.

PRAYERS OF FATIMA

Decade Prayer

Our Lady asked that the following prayer be inserted after each decade of the Rosary:

O my Jesus, forgive us our sins; save us from the fires of hell; lead all souls into heaven, especially those who are in most need of thy mercy.

Sacrifice Prayer

Our Lady taught the children a prayer to be said when they would have something to offer up to God.

O my Jesus, it is for love of You, in reparation for the offenses committed against the Immaculate Heart of Mary, and for the conversion of poor sinners.

Eucharistic Prayer

This prayer stresses that most beautiful truth — that the all-powerful, all-loving God is upon the altar at every Catholic Mass.

Most Holy Trinity, I adore You! My God, my God, I love You in the Most Blessed Sacrament.

The Angel's Prayer

With the Blessed Sacrament suspended in the air, the Angel at Fatima prostrated himself, and recited the prayer:

O most Holy Trinity — Father, Son, and Holy Spirit — I adore thee profoundly. I offer thee the most Precious Body, Blood, Soul, and Divinity of Jesus Christ — present in all the tabernacles of the world — in reparation for the outrages, sacrileges, and indifference by which He is offended. By the infinite merits of the Sacred Heart of Jesus and the Immaculate Heart of Mary, I beg the conversion of poor sinners.

The Pardon Prayer

This was the first prayer taught to the children by the Angel:

My God, I believe, I adore, I trust, and I love thee! I beg pardon for those who do not believe, do not adore, do not trust, and do not love thee.

Notes

1 Robert J. Fox, *Fatima Is Forever* (Hanceville, AL: Fatima Family Apostolate International, 2006), p. 2.

2 Ibid., p. 6.

3 Ibid.

4 Father C. C. Martindale, S.J., *The Message of Fatima* (London: Burns, Oates & Washbourne, 1950), p. 13.

5 Sister Maria Lucia, *"Calls" from the Message of Fatima* (Fatima, Portugal: Secretariado dos Pastorinhos, 2000), p. 60.

6 Martindale, *The Message of Fatima*, p. 17.

7 Robert J. Fox, *Fatima Today* (Front Royal, VA: Christendom Publications, 1983).

8 Sister Maria Lucia, Father Luis Kondor, ed., *Fatima in Lucia's Own Words: Sister Lucia's Memoirs* (Fatima, Portugal: Postulation Centre, 2000).

9 Ibid., p. 78.

10 *The Message of Fatima*, p. 17.

11 Ibid., p. 171.

12 Lucia, Kondor, *Fatima in Lucia's Own Words*, pp. 141–142.

13 Fox, *Fatima Is Forever*, p. 139.

14 Lucia, Kondor, *Fatima in Lucia's Own Words*, p. 81.

15 Ibid.

16 Lucia, Kondor, *Fatima in Lucia's Own Words*, p. 176.

17 Fox, *Fatima Today*, p. 21.

18 Lucia, Kondor, *Fatima in Lucia's Own Words*, p. 176.

19 Lucia, *"Calls" from the Message of Fatima*, p. 58.

20 "Story of Fatima: The Fatima Message in Lucia's Own Words," The Communal First Saturdays website, http://communalfirstsaturdays.org/story-of-fatima/, "The 13th of June, 1917."

21 Fox, *Fatima Today*, p. 24.

22 Luiz Sérgio Solimeo, *Fatima: A Message More Urgent Than Ever* (Spring Grove, PA: America Society for the Defense of Tradition, Family, and Property, 2008).

23 Lucia, Kondor, *Fatima in Lucia's Own Words*, p. 180.

24 Ibid., p. 181.

25 Ibid., p. 182.

26 Ibid.

27 Ibid.

28 Ibid.

29 Ibid.

30 Andrew Apostoli, *Fatima for Today: The Urgent Marian Message of Hope* (San Francisco: Ignatius Press, 2010).

31 "Sixth Apparition of Our Lady," EWTN.com, https://www.ewtn.com/fatima/sixth-apparition-of-our-lady.asp (accessed June 22, 2017).

32 Lucia, *"Calls" from the Message of Fatima*, preface by Father Jesús Castellano Cervera, O.C.D., p. 14.

33 Ibid., p. 98.

34 "What's the Significance of the Fatima Apparitions?" Marians of the Immaculate Conception, http://www.marian.org/fatima/story.php?NID=6956&title=Whats-the-Significance-of-the-Fatima-Apparitions (accessed June 22, 2017).

35 Lucia, Kondor, *Fatima in Lucia's Own Words*, p. 138.

36 Ibid., p. 142.

37 Ibid., p. 156.

38 Ibid., p. 157.

39 Ibid., p. 144.

40 Ibid., p. 148.

41 Ibid., p. 143.

42 João De Marchi, *Mother of Christ Crusade* (Billings, MT: Mother of Christ Crusade, 1947).

43 Lucia, Kondor, *Fatima in Lucia's Own Words*, pp. 164–166.

44 Ibid.

45 Ibid.

46 Fox, *Fatima Is Forever*, p. 114.

47 Lucia, Kondor, *Fatima in Lucia's Own Words*, p. 164.

48 Ibid.

49 Ibid., p. 165.

50 Ibid., p. 166.

51 *Fatima Family Messenger* (A Quarterly Publication of the Fatima Family Apostolate, ed. Robert J. Fox), Jan–March 1989.

52 Fox, *Fatima Today*, p. 90.

53 Ibid., p. 91.

54 Ibid.

55 Ibid., p. 93.

56 Ann Ball, *Young Faces of Holiness: Modern Saints in Photos and Words* (Huntington, IN: Our Sunday Visitor, 2004), p. 77.

57 Lucia, Kondor, *Fatima in Lucia's Own Words*, p. 134.

58 Leo Madigan, *The Children of Fatima: Blessed Francisco; Blessed Jacinta Marto* (Huntington, IN: Our Sunday Visitor, 2000), p. 250.

59 Robert J. Fox, *Documents on Fatima & Memoirs of Sister Lucia: Historical Data, Preface, Pictorial Documentary and Chapters 1–5* (Waite Park, MN: Fatima Family Apostolate and Park Press, Inc., 2002).

60 Ibid.

61 Fox, *Fatima Today*, p. 106.

62 Lucia, Kondor, *Fatima in Lucia's Own Words*, p. 56.

63 Ibid., p. 132.

64 Fox, *Fatima Today*, p. 109.

65 Lucia, Kondor, *Fatima in Lucia's Own Words*, p. 62.

66 Fox, *Fatima Today*, p. 112.

67 Lucia, Kondor, *Fatima in Lucia's Own Words*, pp. 67–69.

68 *Fatima Family Messenger* (A Quarterly Publication of the Fatima Family Apostolate, ed. Robert J. Fox), Jan–March 1990.

69 Ibid.

70 Lucia, Kondor, *Fatima in Lucia's Own Words*, p. 197.

71 "Prioress of Convent Remembers Sister Lucia," Zenit.org. Feb. 21, 2005, https://zenit.org/articles/prioress-of-convent-remembers -sister-lucia/ (accessed May 31, 2017).

72 Ibid.

73 Ibid.

74 Fox, *Fatima Is Forever*.

75 "Prioress of Convent Remembers Sister Lucia," Zenit.org. Feb. 21, 2005, https://zenit.org/articles/prioress-of-convent-remembers -sister-lucia/ (accessed May 31, 2017).

76 Lucia, Kondor, *Fatima in Lucia's Own Words*, p. 198.

77 Ibid.

78 Ibid.

79 Robert J. Fox, "The Power of Mary's Heart to Change the World," Mother of All Peoples website, http://www.motherofallpeoples .com/2005/06/the-power-of-marys-heart-to-change-the-world/ (accessed June 22, 2017).

80 Lucia, Kondor, *Fatima in Lucia's Own Words*, p. 123.

81 Congregation for the Doctrine of the Faith, "The Message of Fatima," Libreria Editrice Vaticana, http://www.vatican.va/ roman_curia/congregations/cfaith/documents/rc_con_cfaith_ doc_20000626_message-fatima_en.html (accessed May 15, 2017).

82 Ibid.

83 Ibid.

84 Pope John Paul II, "Ecumenical Commemoration of the Witnesses to the Faith in the Twentieth Century," par. 4, Libreria Editrice Vaticana, May 7, 2000, https://w2.vatican.va/content/john-paul-ii/ en/homilies/2000/documents/hf_jp-ii_hom_20000507_test-fede .html (accessed June 22, 2017).

85 Congregation for the Doctrine of the Faith, "The Message of Fatima."

86 Ibid.

87 Ibid.

88 Lucia, Kondor, *Fatima in Lucia's Own Words*, pp. 204–205.

89 "The Power of the Rosary," Signs and Wonders website, October 21, 2015, http://www.sign.org/articles/power-rosary (accessed June 22, 2017).

90 Donald H. Calloway, *Champions of the Rosary* (Stockbridge, MA: Marian Press, 2016).

91 Robert J. Fox, *First Saturdays* (Waite Park, MN: Park Press, 2000), p. 11.

92 Lucia, Kondor, *Fatima in Lucia's Own Words*, p. 194.

93 Fox, *Fatima Today*, p. 64.

94 Sister Mary Agatha, CMRI, "The Brown Scapular of Our Lady of Mount Carmel," The Religious Congregation of Mary Immaculate Queen, http://www.cmri.org/05-brown-scapular-of-our-lady-of -mount-carmel.shtml (accessed June 22, 2017).

You might also like ...

Why the Rosary, Why Now?
(ID# T1841)

Using the eloquent and inspiring writings of holy men and women who share a love of the Marian prayer, editor Gretchen R. Crowe makes a compelling case for why praying the Rosary is more critical in today's world than ever before. This is not a typical "how-to" book about the Rosary. It is the "why-to" book that will inspire you to reach for your rosary more often, and in doing so to receive the gifts it offers to each of us and to the world.

Every Day with Mary
(ID# T1867)

Your deeper and more personal relationship with the Blessed Mother can start today with *Every Day with Mary*. Throughout the year you'll ponder Mary's life of peace, love, surrender, hope, gentleness, joy, serenity, self-control, generosity, gratitude, patience, faithfulness, and abundance with a timely and relevant meditation perfect for your busy life.

Available from Our Sunday Visitor:
OSVCatholicBookstore.com
1-800-348-2440